Around the World by Land, Sea and Air

with Mike Harry

AN OXFORDFOLIO PUBLICATION

An Oxfordfolio publication
(www.oxfordfolio.co.uk)

Copyright © Mike Harry 2020

All rights reserved. No part of this publication
may be reproduced, stored in a retrieval system, or
transmitted in any form or by any means, electronic,
mechanical, photocopying, recording, or otherwise,
without the permission of the copyright holder.

Design/typesetting: Forewords
Jacket design: Nick Allen
Project editor: James Harrison

10 9 8 7 6 5 4 3 2 1

A CIP catalogue record for this book is available
from the British Library
ISBN: 978-1-9163099-0-6

Typeset in 11/16 point Adobe Caslon Pro

Printed and bound in the United Kingdom by
Biddles, King's Lynn, Norfolk, UK

Contents

Prologue	vi
Foreword	viii
Friends En Route	xii
Who's Who	xv

Part I: Ten-Pound Pom		1
1	Start of the Journey	3
2	All At Sea	7
3	Land Ahoy!	13
4	Settling In	16
5	Crossing the Nullarbor	20
6	Getting to Know Australia	26
7	Tasmania	31
8	You Should Come Home!	36
9	Into the Unknown	39
10	Taking the Bullet!	43
11	Nagoya, Teruyo and After	46
12	Sayonara Japan	53

CONTENTS

13	The Longest Train Journey in the World!	61
14	The Paris of Siberia	66
15	Moscow Here We Come!	72
16	Coming Home	79
17	Home Sweet Home	82
18	Return to Oz	88
19	Decision Time	92
20	Au Revoir Australia	98
21	Crossing the Pacific and the Atlantic	105
22	Welcome Back Mike!	113
Part II: The Decade of Europe – The 1970s		**117**
23	Back to Rome Again	119
24	No Tulips in Amsterdam and Salad Days	123
25	See Europe in 12 Days	127
26	Mauritian Destiny & Destination South	133
27	The Final Years of the 1970s	139
Part III: Travels and Travails en Famille		**143**
28	The 1980s	145
29	The 1990s – The First Half of the Decade	154
30	The 1990s – The Second Half of the Decade	168

CONTENTS

Part IV: Travels into the New Millennium	**181**
31 New Orleans and the Lost Luggage Saga	183
32 Travelling Again! North-Eastern USA	189
33 The Trans-Canadian	198
34 The End of the Journey	209
Acknowledgements	222

Prologue

This book is the story of a journey that's taken 47 years. It began in 1961 and ended in 2008. It describes a travel milestone which may be unique—one that is the combined journeys around the World by one man (myself), by land, by sea, and by air.

My argument for the uniqueness of the feat goes like this. There are probably millions of people who have actually travelled around the World by plane and that does not just include the crew of aircraft. Furthermore it may be possible that some of those millions might possibly have also travelled around the World by sea. However it is my estimation that the number of people who have circumnavigated the globe both by plane and by sea is probably relatively small. Let us say that there are a few hundred, possibly even a few thousand, who have both flown and sailed around the World. What I think makes my feat unique is that probably none of those thousands will have also circumnavigated the

PROLOGUE

World by land. I may be the only person who has also done this.

So if there is anyone out there who can claim to have circled the World by land, by sea, and by air, please get in touch—maybe we can start our own Round-the-World Club …

Foreword

I have been invited by Mike to pen a foreword for this book in which he shares his experiences, enthusiasm and passion for world travel. Mike has spent a lifetime exploring and engaging with the curious and diverse wonders of this world. His wonderlust started when he visited Rome in 1960 to see the Olympics of that year. The experience of travelling to and from Rome inspired him to travel further afield so in a very short time he quickly made the decision to leave England and test out Australia for possible settlement.

Mike applied to the "Ten-Pound Pom" scheme that had been implemented by the Australian Government to attract English migrants. He left for Australia in 1961.

Australia offered many new challenges being continental size in its own right and the first of those was to see the Empire Games of that year by travelling by train right across Australia from Sydney to Perth and a week later do the return trip from Perth to Sydney. Another big journey a few years later was on a Honda motorcycle from Sydney to Tasmania and back.

New ideas for future travel were developing in his mind including train travel across the Soviet Union, USA and Canada.

I am an Australian born of Greek immigrant parents and I first met Mike in 1963 at the Lane Cove Tennis Club. We shared a lot in common and found that, though we were born on different sides of the world, strangely we were born in the same year, the same month and at what looked like the same time. A long friendship was formed.

Later Mike with two other friends from the club rented a house at number 31, Canberra Avenue, St Leonards. This house became a social hub in which parties, celebrations and card nights were regular events. Anyone could make a pop-in visit. Mike belonged! This became home! He had his tennis and an empathy for Australia.

After eight years in Australia Mike was getting pressure to return to his family so he began to make plans. He realised that the journey home was an opportunity to see new lands so he was delighted when he heard that he could travel to England via Japan, the Soviet Union and Northern Europe. I became inspired by Mike's adventurism

FOREWORD

and aspirations, so when Mike invited me to join him, I did not hesitate, I accepted and resigned my job in the printing industry. We headed off for our five-month trip.

Mike first wrote about that amazing journey in his book *Cast Into the Unknown* where he described our journeys not only on the Japanese Bullet trains but also on the outstanding highlight of the Trans-Siberian Railway during which we experienced hospitality and warmth from locals and rurals. After the end of the Trans-Siberian at Moscow we still continued on by train from Moscow to Warsaw, Berlin, Ostend and finally British Rail to St Albans.

Luton was Mike Harry's home town and a welcome home for the prodigal son was staged. Family reunions followed with siblings, relatives and friends. I became an adopted son in his family. We returned to Australia in mid-September 1970.

In 1971 Mike made the decision to return to the UK, his family and Europe, which is where he remains today. Nevertheless Mike and I remained in close contact through the following decades partly through my regular visits to the UK and Europe.

In 1995 Mike brought his family, Fo, Zoe and Maxim to Australia where they travelled from Perth to Sydney on the Indian Pacific train, and as the new millennium dawned, went on train trips through North-Eastern USA and later on the Trans-Canadian with his son Max—all documented in this book.

But there was more to come! In 2008 while still a young man under 70 years of age Mike, without any thought of taking it easy, undertook a gruelling round the world tour through Thailand, Australia and the USA—again which he recounts in this book.

Mike has clocked up more rail miles and air miles than any other person I know of. It is a grand record! And what's more he maintains his enthusiasm and lust for travel to this day!

Leo Detsikas

Friends En Route

Tony Gomersal, childhood friend

Both Mike and I were born in Luton, on the same street, a few houses apart, in the early years of World War 2. We enjoyed a childhood friendship and forged a close bond that is still going strong today, over 75 years later.

His thirst for travel and adventure emerged when he emigrated to Australia in 1961 staying there for ten years. Since then he has continued travelling across the globe by land, sea and air and he has now written of his exploits.

This new book celebrates Mike's achievement of, he believes, becoming the first person to circumnavigate the globe by all three modes of transport. Well done Mike, I salute you, your friend Tony.

Graham Craik, fellow traveller in the 1970s

It must have been 1971. I was sitting as a nervous student at the start of a Business Studies Course when this athletic looking guy strode in and sat next to me. "Hello Blue" he said in an Aussie accent and from then on "Blue" and "Sport" were born.

Three years later we had got our Business Studies Diplomas and had done some travelling together to Yugoslavia and Italy (white wine and spritzers) and around Amsterdam (herring and beer). For more years than I care to remember, every week, just off Piccadilly, a lot of sweat and calories were expended trying to beat the other one at squash. The Lantern Restaurant provided a welcome postmatch respite.

A lot of water has passed under the bridge since then but our friendship has kept afloat. I still remember meeting Fopin for the first time and I was really proud to be the best man at Mike and Fo's wedding. Our families have now grown up, grandchildren have arrived, and we've retired. We don't cross swords on the court any longer but instead we meet regularly to test the varied London cuisine.

This book is about Mike's life of travel. It has been varied, enquiring and multinational. I am really pleased to have been part of it.

William Karunairajan, the Inspirator

Mike and I were in a programming team more than 40 years ago. Often a few of us would go out for lunch and

Mike would then talk about his travels. He was the most travelled amongst us and it was fascinating listening to him. One could sense his passion and it was at one of these sessions that the idea was born that he should keep records of his travels so that one day he could write about them. I am so happy that he has followed it up and has now produced his second book of travels.

Those of us who know Mike, admire the ease with which he moves within any group of people. It seems true that for any place too, whether in the Australian Outback or the Trans-Siberian Desert, he seems at ease and happy.

Who's Who

Mike Harry	author
Charles Thomas Harry	father of Mike
Doris Harry (née Howard)	mother of Mike

Mike's siblings

Raymond	elder brother
Sylvia	younger sister
Christine	youngest sister

Sylvia's children

Justin	
Adrian	Living in Montreal
Paul	

Fopin	wife of Mike
Popo	mother of Fopin

Fopin's siblings (Fopin was the sixth sibling)

Pierre	Fopin's eldest brother

WHO'S WHO

Sookchin	Fopin's eldest sister
Yangchin	sister of Fopin
Nachin	sister of Fopin
Pengchin	sister of Fopin
Minchoo	sister of Fopin
Mimou	sister of Fopin
Sichin	sister of Fopin
Thaichong	brother of Fopin
Rosemay	friend of Yangchin
Michel	husband of Rosemay
Sandra	friend of Sichin
Iqbal	husband of Sandra

Aussie friends of Mike

Peter Parsons	emigrated to Oz
Sally Parsons	wife of Peter
Laurie Coleman	friend of Mike
Leo Detsikas	friend of Mike
Paul Clarke	emigrated to Oz
Carolyn	wife of Paul
Mike Stephenson	friend of Mike
Paula Stephenson	wife of Mike

Part I

Ten-Pound Pom

1
Start of the Journey

> *... and at any moment the blow might fall, and his chance be gone forever of doing what he had meant to do, of seeing what he had meant to see.*
> Henry Handel Richardson[1]

The journey began on June 8th 1961 at Southampton, England. I was standing on a pier with a Sitmar Line ship towering beside me. Very shortly I would board this boat and it would take me to a strange country on the other side of the world. I did not know it at the time but it was to be the beginning of a journey that would not end until 2008. As I stood there saying farewell to family members I had no idea of what was in front of me and where the journey would take me.

---

[1] My apologies to readers of *Cast Into the Unknown* for reusing this quotation by Australian writer Henry Handel Richardson but it is so perfect.

I was about to leave two wonderful parents, Charles and Doris Harry, also my elder brother Raymond and his family, and two younger sisters, Sylvia and Christine. Also many wonderful aunts, uncles, cousins and friends. I was still only 19. This sea journey was to the other side of the world and would take six weeks, and when I got there I would be in a place where I had no home, no job, no family and no friends. The local population also spoke English in an odd way which I hoped I would be able to understand.

Why was I going on such a journey? Partly because I had developed a passion for travel after a trip with two friends to see the Olympic Games in Rome in 1960. Also I loved the thought of the sun that Australia promised. As a consequence I had responded to an advert I had seen for assisted migration to Australia for just £10. En route there would be accommodation, four meals a day, a gymnasium and even entertainment. Today people pay thousand of pounds to travel on a liner for just two weeks—in 1960 I was being offered six weeks for a mere £10!

START OF THE JOURNEY

Departure day: getting ready to leave on the *Fairsky*

2
All At Sea

*I must go down to the sea again,
to the lonely sea and the sky.*
John Masefield

The ship that was taking me to Australia was called the *Fairsky* and was a ship of the Sitmar Line. Standing beside it at Southampton, it seemed very large to me although by today's massive liner standards it was very modest. There were five decks and I was to find myself in a cabin in the bottom of the boat in E Deck. There was no porthole because E Deck was under water. Although there were six bunks in the cabin there were only three guys: myself, a Scottish guy from Glasgow and a young aspiring pig-farmer from Yorkshire. We discovered that we had an Italian cabin steward called Tony. We were told that if there was anything we needed then we should buzz him. Tony was to do a good job for us during the long voyage ahead.

Up until this time the longest sea journey that I had undertaken was two trips out and back across the Channel when I had gone with friends to Rome in 1960 to see the Olympic Games in that lovely city. And now in complete contrast here I was going to be at sea for over 6 weeks in a voyage of over 12,000 miles! I wondered whether I would get mal-de-mer at some point.

The *Fairsky* passed through the Bay of Biscay then the Straits of Gibraltar, and into the Mediterranean Sea. Eventually, after a number of days travel, the ship berthed at Port Said at the head of the Suez Canal where local traders came to the side of the ship to sell their wares.

When the ship moved off again the Suez Canal provided a route for us to connect the Mediterranean Sea to the Red Sea. As we passed through the Suez Canal we were able to witness camels and palm trees and Egyptians going about their daily life.

However, it was not long before we were in the Red Sea and cruising along the borders of Saudi Arabia to our left and of Sudan to our right. There was one more stop at Aden (now in the Yemen), before we finally emerged into the vast Indian Ocean. Once again traders plied their trade from boats pitched alongside the ship. As we left Aden, Europe was now well behind us and our next stop was going to be in Australia! However, there were many weeks of sailing before we reached the southern continent. It was during this early part of the journey that I turned 20 years of age!

As the ship sailed across the vast Southern Ocean one day passed into another. Some days were really pleasant whilst others could be somewhat boring. We had four meals a day and we could exercise by walking the upper decks or using the small gym or swimming pool. You could sun yourselves but had to be careful not to do it for too long to avoid getting sunburn. In the evening after dinner the tables were moved aside and entertainments were sometimes provided.

There was however some great advantages in being out in the vast ocean, one of which was being able to see the beauty of the endless sea along with occasionally a cloudless blue sky. And just sometimes you glimpsed in the far distance another ship heading towards Europe.

You could make friends from amongst the passengers and it was on this sea journey that I made friends with two English guys called Derek and Robin. I think it was these guys who introduced me to the card games of Canasta and Bridge when the weather kept us inside. Later we were to spend some time together in our early years in Australia.

Eventually the one experience I had hoped not to have, happened. Previously I had never experienced seasickness and I always wondered whether I would gain its acquaintance on this very long journey. And so it was to be. A period eventually came when the ship was said to meet "a slight monsoon". Suddenly the sky became dark and the rain hurtled down and the large liner began to rock in multiple directions. It became very difficult to walk around the ship and walking outside could be dangerous because if you were not careful then you could be sent hurtling over railings and into the turbulent sea.

People began to get sick. Later it was said that 90% of the passengers experienced seasickness and even 70% of the crew. In the end I too succumbed as did my two cabin mates. Nobody turned up for breakfast, lunch or dinner, instead you got your cabin steward, in our case Tony, to bring apples or bread rolls.

However, occasionally I did go out of the cabin. The atmosphere around the ship was weird. Despite the fact that there were probably 2,000 people on the ship, the corridors were completely empty. Strange noises issued from the cabins as you passed them.

Once during the monsoon I made my way to the upper decks and decided to enter the bar. Apart from the barman there was only one customer, a man in his forties or fifties. We talked together about the loneliness we were experiencing because of the mal-de-mer and it was during this conversation that he told me something that thereafter I thanked him for on all my sea journeys. He told me he knew of a cure for sea-sickness, and I believed him, because after all he was perhaps the only person in this ghost ship who seemed to have survived the awful storm. The cure goes as follows. If the sea gets wild, do not go to your cabin, instead go to the bar where you order a strong drink for example a whisky. Sip the whisky steadily, perhaps have more than one. Then if the ship moves in such a way that your stomach goes one way then the whisky will make it move it the other way, and you will remain free of this unpleasant complaint. Since then I have at least twice experienced seas that were even rougher than those I experienced in the Indian Ocean and I have avoided getting seasick on each occasion.

The monsoon lasted two days but eventually the ship left it behind and we moved on to Australia.

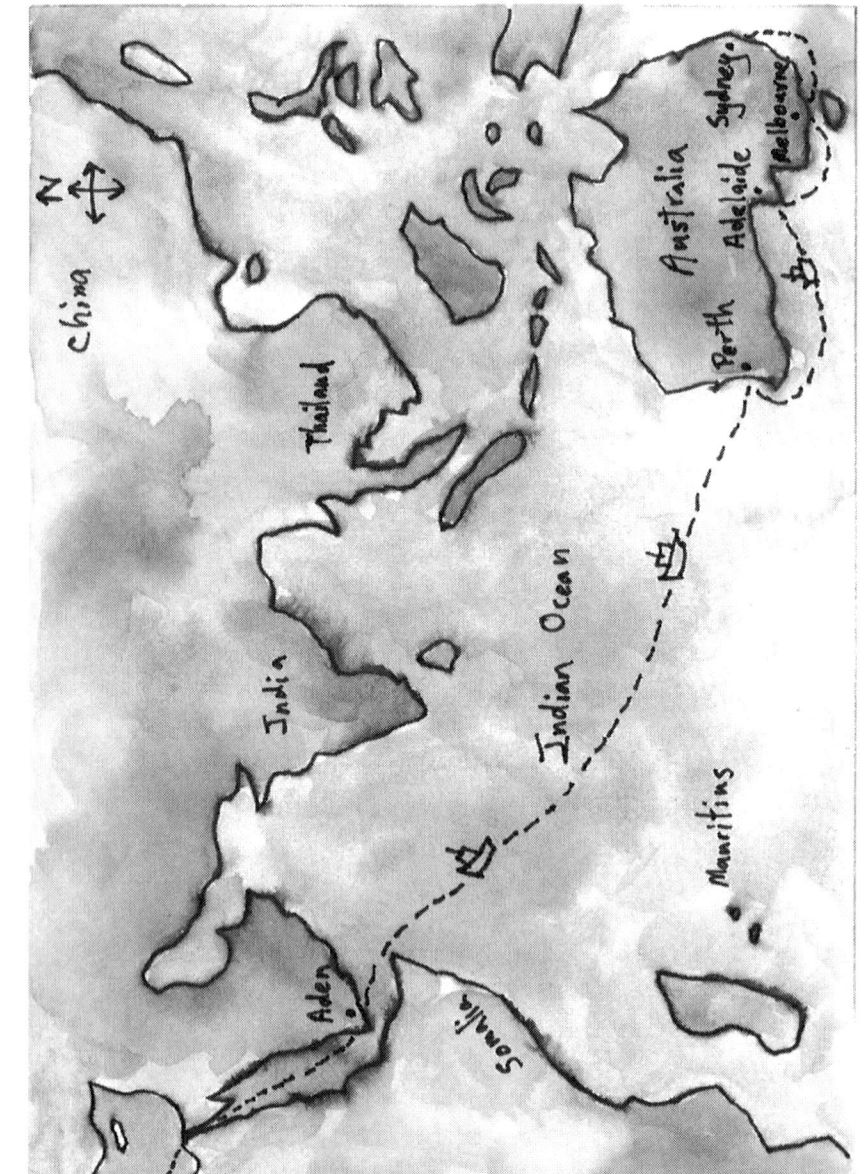

3
Land Ahoy!

*I journeyed far, I journeyed fast; I'm glad I
found the place at last.*
Joel Chandler Harris

I had been at sea five weeks when the *Fairsky* arrived at Fremantle in Western Australia. I could get off there or at any stop the ship made in Australia but I had my mind set on journeying to Sydney to see "that bridge". As a consequence I did not disembark there. Instead I took advantage of the few hours that we were advised the ship would stop in Fremantle to try out my legs on dry land again. The experience was weird because my legs felt rubbery as a result of constantly adjusting my gait for five weeks to the movement of the boat in deep ocean.

After walking a while I found a shop nearby which I thought I would investigate. I went in and saw some Smiths Crisps on the shelves so I asked "could I have some crisps please?" The shopkeeper asked me "do you want some Chips?" "No, not chips" I replied, "I want some crisps". It took some time for me to realise that in Oz they call crisps chips! So, even though it clearly stated crisps on the packet, I eventually walked out of the shop with some chips. I began to think that the Aussies not only sounded strange but they also used English in a different way.

Later I returned to the ship and it moved away from Fremantle first going south before heading east to enter The Great Australian Bight. I still had one more week to reach my destination!

Fortunately despite the reputation of the Bight the journey was relatively smooth and we sailed on with stops at two more cities: Adelaide and Melbourne. Eventually however the ship passed through the Bass Strait before it finally headed north and moved on to my destination—Sydney.

I had been at sea for six long weeks when the *Fairsky* moved inland through the famous Heads and sailed onward along one of the most beautiful natural harbours in the world. En route we passed a place with a really weird name, it had eight "O"s in it Woolloomooloo!! Increasingly I began to wonder what I had let myself in for.

Suddenly there was that bridge, looking absolutely amazing, The Sydney Harbour Bridge. I was to get to know

LAND AHOY!

it very well in future years but on first viewing it took my breath away. (The famous Opera House had yet to be built.)

We passed the beautiful Royal Botanic Gardens on the left before finally sailing under "that bridge" and turning to port to park the *Fairsky* in a berth in what I later learned was called Pyrmont. **I had finally arrived after six weeks sailing halfway around the world** to a city that was to be my home for the next ten years! I was both nervous and eager with anticipation.

4
Settling In

My home, the city, and the image of well-known places pass before my eyes.
Ovid

In the next year I tried to adapt to living in a new country away from all my family and friends. The first need was of course to find somewhere to live. I, along with all other migrants, had been told that the Immigration Department could arrange some accommodation for us. We had been told we could choose from either barrack buildings or private lodgings. I chose the latter, and when asked where I would like the lodgings to be I answered Bondi Beach, the beach that I had seen in many photos back in England. I was told that they could find lodgings for me in Bondi Village up the hill above the beach. I agreed and I was taken from the *Fairsky* to there by a taxi truck provided for me. When I got there I found that I had to share my room

SETTLING IN

with a young mechanic. He seemed a friendly guy and I settled in with my five cases of belongings.

However, I was not to be in Bondi Village for long, as my two friends from the boat, Robin and Derek, lived nearby and within three weeks we decided that we would find a house which we could share together. As a consequence we three eventually moved to another suburb called Double Bay. These two addresses were to be the first of 14 addresses that I was to have in the next five years before finally I settled down in a beautiful bungalow in St Leonards.

The next need was to find a job to pay for our rent, food and many other expenses. On the boat we had been told

Sydney home

that we were going to Australia at a period during which Australia was experiencing the worst depression since the awful 1930s. So after a couple of weeks sightseeing around Sydney, we three young fellows decided that perhaps we should heed what we had been told and go to enrol for the dole.

So we three went to the local Social Security Office on a Wednesday. Derek got a job that day in a photographic organisation. Unfortunately he had an argument with the boss very early and was laid off by the end of the week. I was sent for an interview at WD and HO Wills (Australia) Limited and received an offer of employment on the Friday. I was to work for that organisation for 27 months.

Robin was not as fortunate as Derek and I and it took him nine months before he was offered work at New South Wales State Mines at the time when they were setting up a computer unit. However much later when I said farewell to him nine years later he was the head of the Computing Department!!

Very important too was to find how to satisfy my enormous appetite. I had been brought up with a mother who could cook the most amazing meals and she provided me with sustenance at breakfast, lunch and dinner. Suddenly she wasn't there and I had to sort out my own meals. I

SETTLING IN

could make bacon and eggs and boil an egg. Other than that it was possible for me to buy food from local restaurants such as curries, Chinese food and fish and chips, but of course all this cost money. To eat better I wrote letters to my mother and to my Aunt Eva asking them to send me recipes. When the recipes eventually arrived I began to learn how to cook. However, this was to take weeks as the only way to communicate from England to Australia and vice-versa in those days was by letters and this would take five days each way! Anyway meals did eventually start to improve.

5

Crossing the Nullarbor

All sunshine and nothing else makes a desert.
Charles Haddon Spurgeon

In 1960 I had travelled to Rome with two friends to see the Olympic Games of that year. This was to be a wonderful experience in so many ways. We did for instance manage to see a great deal of amazing sport including watching a young American boxer called Cassius Clay win the light-heavyweight boxing title. Apart from the great sport that we enjoyed watching we were also able to see the completely different living environments that existed in France, Italy and Switzerland. Nevertheless the most fundamental experience for me was to enjoy the journey so much that travel had became an obsession!

Rome 1960 was a major influence in my decision to travel to Australia and I now found myself in a country which was going to host the 1962 Empire Games in a city called Perth. I decided that I should go and see these Games. The first shock was to realise how far Perth was from Sydney—a massive 2,431 miles which was like travelling across the whole of Europe! I could always fly and be there within hours, but I did not consider this possibility because I wanted to see Australia close-up. As a consequence I decided to travel by rail. The second shock was to learn that it would take seven days to get there!

The reason for the great length of time involved in travelling from Sydney in New South Wales to Perth in Western Australia was the fact that the history of railway development in Oz involved decisions that led to different railway gauges in the different States as these States were formed. Thus the gauge in New South Wales was 4′8½″, 5′3″ in Victoria and South Australia, and amazingly a mere 3′6″ in Western Australia. Nevertheless, despite the great length of the journey, I decided I would prefer to see Australia up close.

The train left Sydney Central Railway Station and moved south to the New South Wales – Victoria border at Albury where to my amazement I had to gather my luggage together and walk with it down the long platform to another train that could be seen further on. The new train of course was in Victoria and sitting on a 5′3″ gauge track.

As the train moved through Victoria we passed from day into night. At one point a rather scary looking man entered the carriage that I was in and decided we needed entertaining. He told us that he was very happy because he had just been let out of prison and wanted to share his happiness with us by singing songs to us, his fellow passengers! As a consequence we were regaled by many songs, sung in a very loud voice. No one felt brave enough to complain and few of us slept!

We eventually arrived at Melbourne, the capital of Victoria, where I had to disembark and wait for most of the day before catching my third train that would take me on to Adelaide, the capital of the State Of South Australia. When I eventually got to Adelaide I had to change trains again to get a fourth train that took me through Port Pirie and on to Port Augusta.

Something changed at Port Augusta however because the fifth train that I boarded was run by Commonwealth Railways on the standard 4'8½" gauge and this train was scheduled to transport me for a vast distance through an area called the Nullarbor Desert.

I had no comprehension of what I was about to see. The train across the Nullarbor was going to travel for 1,051 miles until it arrived at an historic town called Kalgoorlie.

CROSSING THE NULLARBOR

On this train I had the advantage of a sleeping berth which was great after the seats that I had had to put up with on the journey so far. What was weird however was waking up one morning after another and looking out of the window to see how the scenery had changed – only to find it hadn't! The Nullarbor seemed to have been planted with plants that I was informed were spinefex and saltbush. Each morning, and all day long, you could look out and see these plants seemingly extending in straight lines into the distance. The place was awesomely empty. In all the time I travelled across the desert I never saw any sort of human or animal life. Nevertheless I was assured that not only the indigenous aboriginal people, but also kangaroos and dingoes could be found there.

The only habitation across the Nullarbor were small townships whose existence was only to service the Trans Australian Railway. Also just out of Port Pirie a piece of track begins that extends in a non-deviating straight line for 297 miles—that must do something to a train driver's vision!

Finally, however, we arrived in the evening at a town called Kalgoorlie which had been established in 1893 following the discovery of gold in the local area. The place looks entirely different now, but in 1962 Kalgoorlie was like a USA frontier town with dirt roads leading from the station and saloons with doors that you push open just as in the cowboy films. It was still 400 miles from Perth, the capital of Western Australia,

We only had a few hours to get a drink and nourishment before we had to go back to the station to board our sixth train. This proved to be a weird experience because the gauge changed to 3′6″ which meant that as the train moved along the 400 miles to Perth the wide carriages seemed to rock dangerously up and down.

Eventually, however, we arrived in Perth. The journey from Sydney had taken seven days but I wouldn't have missed a minute of it. I now knew what the vast interior of Oz was like and its memory never fades!

I stopped in Perth for another seven days sleeping in a tent on Fremantle Football Ground. Each morning I travelled to the stadium to watch the Empire Games, mainly the athletics and swimming.

Perth is said to be one of the sunniest cities in the world and I was to experience such a lot of the sun there that virtually my whole skin peeled off there whilst I watched the Games. In the years that followed I learnt to be more sensible when exposing my body to hot sun.

I had spent a week getting to Perth, then a week

watching the Games, and then finally spending another week travelling back to Sydney. Strangely as a result of this experience I found that I loved long journeys by train. This was just as well as I was to do even longer journeys in the future! 33 years later, in 1995, I persuaded my wife Fopin and our two children, Zoe and Maxim, to join me in travelling across Australia on the Indian Pacific train from Perth to Sydney. This time the journey was to last only 68 hours because they were using a single gauge. Even so, there were still some grumbles that it took far too long!

6

Getting to Know Australia

He that travels far knows much.
Proverb

In 1962 I purchased myself a small 50cc Honda motorcycle mainly to get me to and from work and for other journeys around Sydney. However in the next six plus years this bike was really put to the test as it got used not only to get me familiar with the State of New South Wales and the Australian Capital Territory but also for travel much further afield.

Early in 1966 I decided to drive the Honda from Sydney to Brisbane and back as a warm-up for a much longer trip that was to come. On the carriage rack at the rear of the bike I strapped my haversack and a tent whilst all the rest of the gear that I needed was placed in the two panniers. The 613-mile journey to Brisbane goes mainly along the coast and takes you through Newcastle, Port MacQuarie

GETTING TO KNOW AUSTRALIA

My Honda motorcycle in Brisbane

and Coffs Harbour. The scenery en route was spectacular and the whole journey there and back took me one week.

Having finished the warm-up ride I started to prepare for the much longer ride which was to take me south of Sydney through New South Wales and Victoria to Melbourne where I was to catch a ferry to the island State of Tasmania.

I left on Saturday morning and drove to a place called Kangaroo Valley where I found myself sharing the youth hostel with a large group of Irish youth hostellers. They were a very friendly bunch and they invited me to join them through the weekend which included Saturday night

A beautiful view between Brisbane and Sydney

in the local pub and Sunday swimming in a nearby beautiful water hole.

Come Monday however it was time to move on and I loaded my bike up for departure. I was considerably concerned when the bike seemed reluctant to start. Was my trip going to end at Kangaroo Valley? But no, suddenly the engine roared into life, and I was then able to say farewell to my Irish friends and drive off.

Melbourne is 596 miles from Sydney so I made one further stop en route at a motel in Yass.

In Melbourne I had been invited to stay at the house

GETTING TO KNOW AUSTRALIA

Flinders Street Railway Station in Melbourne

of Dave and Ann Bracey. This came about as a result of an amazing coincidence. Some three years earlier in Sydney I had been returning from some evening classes and walking up the steep road called William Street when I saw a couple walking down the hill towards me. As we got closer I become more and more convinced that I knew the man. When we drew close there was mutual recognition. I had known Dave at Luton Grammar School. He was a couple of years older than me but we had competed together in the school teams of cross-country and rugby union. He and Ann had only just arrived in Sydney that day and were stopping on for just the one night in Kings Cross before leaving Sydney and flying on to Melbourne the next day. The coincidence of our meeting was extraordinary. That evening we dined together and exchanged addresses. Three years later I joined them in Melbourne.

After a few very pleasant days with them, my Honda and I headed for the ferry and set off for the island of Tasmania.

Tasmania coming into view

7

Tasmania

A prison in a prison.
Charles Dickens

Tasmania was full of experiences. I was planning a clockwise circular route around the island but first of all after landing I drove west along the north coast to see the headland with the odd name of The Nut. After seeing The Nut I turned the bike around and headed east again to stop at a youth hostel beside the tallest mountain in Tasmania. The next morning I joined other hostellers and climbed to the top of this mountain. At the top we separated and I found myself coming down the mountain on my own. However, I was a little unnerved when I saw a small black snake crossing the path in front of me as I had heard that Tasmania had some of the most venomous and dangerous snakes in the world and some of these were small and black. I waited until it had disappeared off to my left before moving on down the path.

Soon after the descent from the mountain I got on my motorcycle and continued driving to the east before following the road as it turned in a southwards direction.

As I drove Tasmania reminded me very much of England because it was green and undulating. En route I stopped at youth hostels in Scamander and Bicheno before arriving at the Orford Hostel. Luckily I was the first there and was able to book a bunk for myself before a large group arrived from Hobart the island capital. Because of the size of the group some of these folks, both guys and gals, would have to sleep on the floor. They were there for a party and I was invited to join them beginning with a visit to a pub. A good time was had by all and eventually we retired for sleep.

During the night I had to obey the call of nature and headed for the toilet which unfortunately was outside across a rear lawn. Nature satisfied I headed back to the hostel when calamitously my foot discovered some broken glass in the grass. I hobbled as best as I could back into the hostel with my foot bleeding profusely and tried to wake one of the sleeping bodies on the floor. The person berated me "I'm sleeping!" but fortunately someone else had noticed that I was in trouble and called out "this guy is bleeding!"

TASMANIA

Soon the whole hostel was awake, emergency repairs were undertaken, and I was then driven by car to a nearby hospital for anaesthetics and stitches. Later I was brought back to the hostel where I managed to get some sleep.

The next morning amazingly enough I felt fine and I was able to get onto my Honda and drive off with the good wishes of my fellow hostellers sending me on my way. The hospital's work had been good and I amazingly had no problem with the wound.

The next stop on the journey through Tasmania was Port Arthur, a place that I was anticipating greatly because it was in the prison there that the British had sent their most dangerous prisoners to be held.

As stated earlier Tasmanian hostels were usually well populated, both on the way to Port Arthur and also later on the way north from Port Arthur. Thus I was very surprised when I discovered that I was to be the only person sleeping at the Port Arthur youth hostel that night. I collected the key from the local shopkeeper and made my way to the wooden hostel. I discovered it consisted of a central community area with men and women's dormitories to either side. It was February 14th 1966. I think that this was the day that decimal currency was introduced to Australia, however I remember it for something different!!

That evening I spent a few pleasant hours in the local hostelry before returning to the hostel. I cannot remember when I learned it, but at some time I had learned that the hostel that I was about to sleep in had once been where the Irish political prisoner William Smith O'Brien had been imprisoned. He had been held in isolation from the other prisoners as they feared he would encourage them to rebel. After many years of imprisonment, O'Brien was finally allowed to return to Ireland but I can imagine that night after night, year after year, this man must have hated the lonely nights he was forced to spend in that solitary hut.

Well that was his time but now it was my time to be there. As is my habit I read a little before heading for my lonely bunk in the men's dorm. I turned out the light and prepared myself for sleep. Suddenly however I heard a noise, it was a shuffling noise so I got out of bed to investigate the central area thinking I had left something open. I found the dorm completely secure so I returned to my bunk. However, I had not been there very long before the noise came again. I got out of bed a second time, and this time checked outside the hostel under the verandah where my bike was parked to see if there were any small animals hiding there (there were none!) and also to see if the branches of the tree I remember having seen were brushing the roof (The tree was too far away!). Satisfied once more that there was no explanation for the noise I returned to bed. Needless to say the noise came back again. The sound was just like the sound you would get when a man walks across the floor of the hut, stops on the other side, and then walks back! Hoping everything would be alright in the morning, I told myself to ignore any further disturbance and go to sleep.

The next day I decided to leave Port Arthur rather than risk another night of foot shuffling. Instead I visited the capital Hobart before going on to a hostel in New Norfolk where to my delight I was joined by two attractive English girls who had just hiked down the centre of the island. We had food and drinks together at the local hostelry and the next day I left them to drive up the centre of the island. En route I stopped at two more hostels at both of which I had the company of fellow hostellers. Continuing to the northern coast I caught the ferry from Devonport to Melbourne and from there returned to Sydney.

8

You Should Come Home!

Be it ever so humble, there's no place like home.
John Howard Payne

By July 1968 I had been in Australia seven years. Perhaps I was so busy enjoying myself so much that I hadn't noticed the rapid passing of time. However, it was in that month that I was informed very firmly that I should make a return journey to the UK.

Time had passed much slower for my family and especially perhaps for my mother. I received a letter at that time from my Aunt Alice, one of Mum's sisters and luckily for me the Aunt who had agreed to be my guardian. She advised me that my mother was missing me very much. Although she would have loved to travel to Australia to see me, Australia was a very great distance away requiring multiple aeroplanes to get there from the UK at the time. To complicate matters she was a very poor traveller who got sick in a mere car journey from Bedfordshire to Cornwall.

Aunt Alice went on to explain that my mother would not tell me how sad she was because she did not want to put any pressure on me. However, my Aunt told me very clearly that she herself felt no such reservation and because of this she was going to tell me exactly what I should do. I should decide what year I would be able to come back to England and then let my mother know when she would see me. My mother would be happy with that my Aunt said, and then as an afterthought added "And so would I!

Aunt Alice was, apart from being a wonderful lady, very strong-minded who couldn't be argued with, so I told her I would do exactly as she recommended.

From that point on therefore I began to make plans for a return trip to England. I could of course fly back to England within two days. However plane travel is relatively boring as you see so little apart from clouds. I looked for a far more interesting way to travel home. Then I saw it! A local travel agent called Orbit Travel Service was advertising a new trip that was now possible—journeying on the Trans-Siberian Railway through the Soviet Union. This would be amazing way to journey home so I told the travel agent to make the necessary arrangements.

Then I had some good luck. My close friend Leo Detsikas said that he could get long-service-leave from his employer and would be very happy to join me. Great news! From that point on we made arrangements for this very long journey together.

Some friends who heard about our plans tried to put us off attempting this trip. Japan and the USSR were very alien cultures to Oz we were told, and also people disappeared in the USSR. Also at the time there was a so-called "Cold War" between the communist countries and the western countries. And to make matters worse there was something of a hot war dispute between China and the USSR over their common border. However despite these concerns Leo and I remained determined.

9

Into the Unknown

He delighted to wander in unknown places to see unknown rivers.
Ovid

The next week was going to be an amazing experience even before we got to Japan and the Soviet Union.

I did not behave particularly sensibly before takeoff as I spent most of the night before the flight with three friends before heading for Kingston Smith Airport at about four o'clock in the morning. At the airport we had a breakfast and awaited the 20 to 30 friends who were coming to see Leo and I off and say farewell to us (not literally I hoped).

The journey by plane to Japan was going to be a massive new experience as the total journey time was nearly a whole day, and the longest airplane flight I had ever taken up until then was from London to Paris a journey that was almost over as soon as it had begun!

Having said goodbye to our friends at the airport the Japan Air Line plane was soon flying out of Sydney and heading north. Even so it would be a long time before we left the Australian mainland behind as the country I had lived in since 1961 was such a vast area. One pleasant experience though was being offered breakfast by beautiful stewardesses dressed in kimonos.

After we had finally said cheerio to Oz our first landing was at Manila, the capital of Philippines. The landing was a very unpleasant experience for me, however, because I suffered a sharp pain in my ears, possibly a punishment for my stopping out all night rather than sleeping.

Manila airport

INTO THE UNKNOWN

We were able to get off the plane there and head for the Intransit Lounge for cold drinks which were very welcome because out on the tarmac the heat was intense, which we felt especially as we were dressed in suits! Somewhat worrying however was the fact that there had been riots in Manila just before we had arrived, and even part of the airport had been bombed. We wondered whether there was going to be a repeat bombing but it wasn't to be, and soon we were back on the plane and on our way to our second stop, romantic Hong Kong.

Hong Kong now has one of the largest and most modern airports in the world but in 1970 the airport was very small with the wall of a mountain at the end of the runway! The worst possibility for me was my concern that the plane would not be able to stop and consequently slam into the mountain. And that concern was on top of the repeat pain in my ears! Thankfully the pilot brought the plane safely down. Leo and I had planned to stop for a few days at Hong Kong when we returned to Oz in a couple of months time. However on this day we were only able to look at the Hong Kong skyline from the transit lounge. After one hour we were called back to the plane which then set off on the third section of the journey, to Japan!

This was not going to be such a long flight and soon we

were informed that we were about to land in Tokyo. Once more the pain in the ears, the worst pain of the day, spoilt the landing for me.

What would Japan be like? For the first time I would be in a country where the whole population was of a different ethnic type to my own. We had also moved from the last days of autumn in the southern hemisphere to the first days of summer in the northern hemisphere!! Weird or what!?

10
Taking the Bullet!

Imagination is a doorway to a world where dreams come true.
Anon

Japan was going to be an immense experience for us both. It began on our journey by hotel bus to our hotel! At that time Tokyo had the reputation of having the worst traffic jams in the world and even though it was now very late at night the traffic on the roads was still dense.

The second surprise was our hotel! When our travel agent Marian had booked it for us I thought that the Palace Hotel seemed a nice name but when I got to Tokyo I found out why it had got it's name. The Australian dollars bought a lot of yen in 1970 and our hotel was not only luxurious but it was just across the road from the palace of the Japanese Emperor! The next morning, after a wonderful sleep, we found we could look across the road into the back garden of the Emperor's palace. We looked to see if the Emperor was taking a morning constitutional but unfortunately he was nowhere to be seen.

After a good breakfast Leo and I first went out shopping. I had arrived in Tokyo with two suitcases but I thought I would need more as I expected to buy plenty of souvenirs and gifts for my family. As a consequence, I decided to buy a very large black bag and a portable radio.

After shopping, we went out to see what the Tokyo street life was like. The people looked a lot different to us Aussies both physically and in clothing. Not only was the language completely strange to us but only a few people spoke English so we had to playact to get around. Also we were constantly finding something different to anything that we had seen, heard, or felt before. Buildings were different, sometimes there were smells that were completely alien to us, and then there was the noise and the traffic jams! In the end, the walking, traffic and the noise made us feel very tired so we returned to our hotel for the night, this time the Hotel Okura. Tomorrow we were leaving Tokyo!

In my last job at The Bureau Of Census and Statistics one of the ladies in my team, whose name alas I now cannot recall, after hearing that I was heading for Japan, asked if I would like an introduction to a young woman called Teruyo who had been living with her and her family whilst she studied in Sydney. Naturally I said I would be delighted to and so it was that tomorrow Leo and I were to catch a train to a city called Nagoya, some 400 km from Tokyo.

We were to travel to Nagoya on a train given the unusual name of "bullet". Perhaps this was because these trains were as fast as a bullet! I had heard about these trains for a few years and their ability to travel between Japanese cities at an average speed of 100+ miles an hour. As the train stood at the platform it looked very small. Nevertheless we boarded it and were able to make ourselves comfortable. Shortly afterwards, without us realising it had happened, the train left the platform and we were soon flashing past houses, cars and trees at an unbelievable speed. Nagoya here we come!

11
Nagoya, Teruyo and After

Welcome ever smiles, and farewell goes out sighing.
William Shakespeare

Within a few hours we had arrived at Nagoya where I telephoned Teruyo at her office. She told me that we should take a taxi to the City Hall where she worked and then she would meet us there.

We found Teruyo outside waiting to greet us at the City Hall. She said that she would have to work until late in the afternoon but if we left our luggage with her then she would store it in a safe place whilst we were sightseeing Nagoya. Also when we returned at 5 pm she would then be fully at our service. She said that during the evening there were two alternatives for us to choose from, she could either take us out and show us Nagoya, or we could come to her home and spend the evening with her and her family.

NAGOYA, TERUYO AND AFTER

Nagoya Town Hall

Leo and I had only a brief discussion before telling Teruyo that seeing her Japanese home from the inside was a much more interesting proposition. We then said adieu while we went off to see Nagoya Castle.

At the designated time we returned to the City Hall to find Teruyo waiting for us with her boss who delighted us by giving us gifts of tie clips that showed a sea dragon, the symbol of Nagoya. He also informed us that that the City Hall was laying on a car to convey us and Teruyo to her home. We were amazed at the hospitality we were receiving. We were even more staggered when a large limousine drew up and we were invited to board.

As we drove into the suburbs we became more appreciative of the gift of the limousine because we noticed that the buses were packed and the traffic was horrendous. We tried to imagine what it would have been like if instead we had had to make our way on the bus with the quantity of luggage that we had.

Eventually we reached Teruyo's home which surprised us because it was a large two-storey building situated in a relatively empty street. We understood that most people in Japan lived in flats. As the limousine stopped Teruyo's parents came out to greet us and invited us to come into their house. As we moved through the front entrance we

Teruyo's home in Nagoya

discovered that first there was a soil area which we had to step up from to move onto a wooden floor. Before stepping up onto the wood we had to remove our shoes. Shortly after we were introduced Teruyo's two sisters who giggled as we met!

We were then informed by Teruyo that a meal was being prepared for us but in the meantime she thought perhaps we would like to take a bath. Leo and I both felt sweaty from the day's exertions so we immediately replied yes with enthusiasm. However, we were a little taken aback when Teruyo said "You know we bath differently here in Japan to the way you do in Australia?" What on earth did she mean? Did everybody have a communal bath? No that was not how it was done. She showed us a large wooden box full of hot, clean water in a small bathroom. The first to use it was the father, followed by the guests, then the next oldest male in the family, then the remaining males, finally all the females starting with the oldest. Leo and I were staggered when we heard this but each of us wanted to be the first to use the water before the other. We decided to toss for it and happily I won!

Teruyo then told us how to bath. Inside the bathroom there was a wooden platform where you stood as you took a bowl of water from the box. You washed your body with soap in this water before throwing the water away. You then took another bowl of water to cleanse your body of soap. Finally you climbed into the box and soaked in the hot, clean water. When I finally got out of the box, got dressed and left the bathroom, Leo had the cheek to mutter "I hope you have left the water clean!"

After we had our baths we were informed dinner was ready but in fact it was more like a feast. Since Teruyo's father had retired from the Nagoya Fire Force he had apparently become a sushi cook so that night, as well as sushi, we enjoyed soup, tempura and many different rice meals, washed down with beer, whisky, saki wine and green tea.

When the meal was over we were all sleepy so bedtime called. The dinner had been held upstairs and we were surprised to be told that we would also be sleeping there. We were even more surprised to be informed that the three girls would be sleeping there also. What happened after everything was taken away was that the father pulled a screen across the floor, the three girls slept on one side, we two on the other. We looked for the beds but couldn't see any. Then we were introduced to futons. Leo and I went to sleep with the girls giggling on the other side of the screen.

The next day we thanked our hosts profusely and

Daibutso Temple, Nara

accompanied Teruyo on her bus to City Hall. She had timed the bus to avoid the peak time so, although it was still crowded, the journey was bearable despite our luggage.

After we said farewell to Teruyo we took a train to see Nara which had been the capital of Japan between 710 and 784 AD. At Nara we were able to see the Daibutso which is a colossal image of Buddha and said to be the largest statue in the world housed in the largest wooden structure in the world.

After Nara, we travelled to Kyoto which had also been a capital of Japan—from 794 to 1868 AD. We stopped there one night in our first Japanese Inn where once more we were confronted with the box bath. This time the shock was not so great.

The next day we returned by a "bullet" train to Tokyo and made our way to our last Japanese hotel, the Hotel New Japan. We had to prepare for our departure from Japan and our journey to the Soviet Union!

12

Sayonara Japan

There's the old sea welcome waiting for you.
Captain Ronald Hopwood

The next morning we had to say "sayonara" to fascinating Japan. Thankfully, as it turned out, we gave ourselves plenty of time to get to the port and left the hotel by a taxi to the nearest railway station where we had to get a train to the Port of Yokahama.

When we entered the station it seemed quiet enough and we were about to descend a long flight of stairs to our platform when a train arrived at the platform and suddenly hundreds of people descended from the train and started to rush to the stairs that we were standing on. We decided that it was tactful to stop where we were and let them pass.

When the stairs were clear we moved down the stairs and waited for the next train. At that time the platform itself was not overcrowded. However another train arrived and we could see that the train seemed packed with apparently no standing room left. Because of this we were amazed at what we saw next! Despite the train appearing fully packed most of the people on the platform still decided that they must board it! We were even more shocked when we saw railway staff on the platform literally pushing people onto the train!!

Having seen this Leo and I decided that the amount of luggage that we had would make getting on the train difficult, if not impossible. Consequently we waited as first one more train came in, then another, with the same amazing scenes as before. After watching three trains going through our platform without us being able to board we began to worry about the possibility of missing our ship at Yokohama. We decided to ask a smart looking young gentleman if he could tell us when a train would arrive that we would be able to board. His English was good and he informed us not to get on the next train, nor the train after that, but to get on the train after that.

We did exactly what the gentleman said, and watched unbelievingly as the scenes we had earlier seen were repeated on the next two trains. This made us apprehensive about the third train he had suggested we board but in the outcome he was perfectly correct as it arrived with masses of room! The rush hour was over!

The *Khabarovsk*

The train took us to the Yokohama Port and we found the boat that was going to take us to the Soviet Union. It was called the MV *Khabarovsk*. We boarded the boat and were directed to our cabins. For some reason although I had booked first, Leo got a cabin on an upper deck and I got a cabin on the bottom deck. Shades of the *Fairsky*!

My cabin had four bunks but there were just three of us. Myself, plus two young fellows from Canada called Mike and Ari. One of them, I cannot remember who now, had been born in the Soviet Union but had gone with his parents to Canada decades earlier.

It wasn't long before the boat got under way. Having stored my luggage I went looking for Leo. I found him on Deck 3 in a cabin with two young ladies. Lucky fellow I thought. One of the lassies was an attractive young woman called Megan who had been born in Wales but was now an Australian and she was now going back to Wales to check out her roots. Having introduced me to Megan, Leo then pointed to the top bunk and indicated that the young lady there was not feeling very well because the sea was very rough and the movement of the ship upset her.

We didn't see the young lady in the bunk that day because of the mal-de-mer, but by the second day the *Khabarovsk* had sailed around the north of Japan, then south into the calmer Sea of Japan which lies between Japan and the Soviet Union. With the calmer seas I was able to meet the young lady who was Japanese and called Shinako and seemed to be a talented young woman because she was going to Scandinavia to study music. Later that day she played the piano and we all had a sing-song.

After three days sailing we arrived at the Soviet port of Nachhodka which was to be our port of disembarkation. But first we had to meet the Soviet Customs staff. Two men entered my cabin and quickly processed my Canadian cabin mates. Then they turned to me and spoke to me in

Megan and Shinako

Yours truly, Shinako, Leo and Megan

Russian. My cabin mate explained that I had been asked to point out my luggage. Of course I had a lot. I pointed out the three suitcases and they asked me to open them all. They looked through all three of them in great detail putting a few things aside to ask me about later. One of them was a copy of Playboy that I had borrowed from Leo. They looked at the photos of the young women without smiling or commenting. Then there was an economics textbook which puzzled them. There was also a box containing 150 slides that I was taking back to show my family. Amazingly, the guy looked through all of them! Eventually however they were finished having found nothing incriminating,

Looking for my luggage unloaded from the ship

they mumbled something and left. That was my welcome to the USSR!

When we disembarked there was a train waiting for us and our luggage was brought to the train in ancient lorries. This train was to take us on an overnight journey of 12 to 15 hours to the city of Khabarovsk some 910 km away. At Khabarovsk we were to board the train that would take us on the longest train journey in the world, the Trans-Siberian!

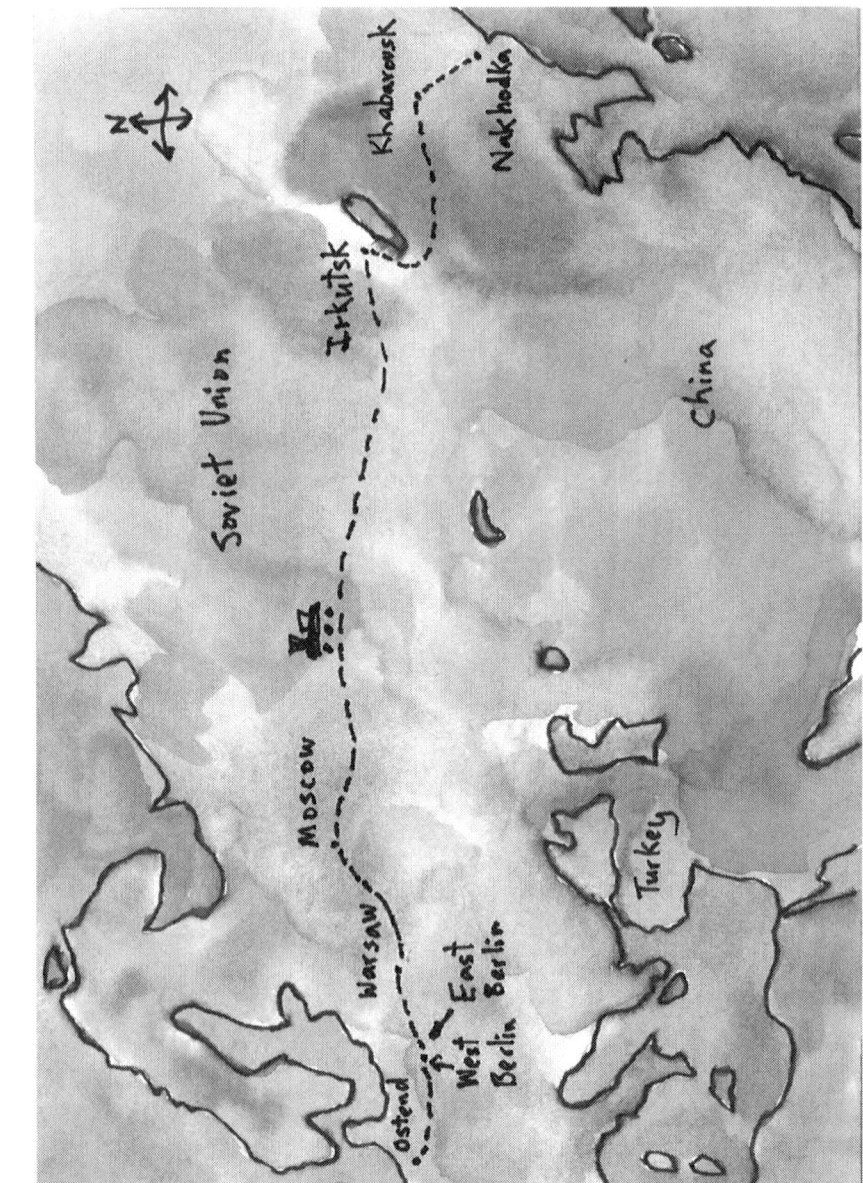

13

The Longest Train Journey in the World!

Railroads are the interfusers of mankind, and will hasten their improvement more than even printing has done.
G. T. De Wilde

Khabarovsk was a cold and grey place but it was here that we were to board a train that would take us on a journey of 8,531-km to Moscow. This distance made the Sydney to Perth rail journey seem a relative minnow.

First of all though we had to say cheerio to Shinako who was flying to Scandinavia via Moscow. Although we had only known each other for three days we had begun a friendship which was to last right up to the present time. After studying music in Scandinavia she moved to Paris where she became an artist and also met and fell in love with a Japanese gentleman called Ken.

Travelling in the USSR was a unique experience one part of it being the surveillance of a Soviet tourist organisation called Intourist. From the time we booked our tickets in Sydney we found Intourist required to know exactly where we would be on every day that we were in the USSR. It would book all our hotels and provide us with vouchers to cover all our meals on the trains.

Soon after leaving Khabarovsk we could see some mountains approximately seven miles away. These mountains were the Chinese border and only months earlier China and the USSR had been shelling each other in this area in a border dispute. We were glad when we left the mountains behind without being involved in a renewal of the shelling.

As the train moved on we were able to discover that the foreigners on the train were very much a minority, probably no more than 20. The largest group were surprisingly German. In addition there was a New Zealand couple, some Australians including Leo, Megan and myself, an American called Bob, and one young Japanese guy called Yuji who was heading for Berlin.

We had not travelled very far before we saw Yuji walking back to us looking particularly nervous. We asked him what the problem was. He explained that he had met some

THE LONGEST TRAIN JOURNEY IN THE WORLD!

Russians in the train corridors who said to him "We don't like you people". Whether it was because Yuji was Japanese or whether it was because they thought he was Chinese Yuji didn't know. We attempted to reassure Yuji and told him to stick close to us and not to wander off on his known.

The train would stop about four times a day. You could anticipate a forthcoming stop when you saw the Russian passengers get out of their pyjamas, put on their shoes, and move into the corridors. The train usually only stopped for about 20 minutes. As a consequence the moment the doors were opened passengers quickly alighted, some running off to nearby buildings, others going to check out the merchandise that was being sold on tables placed along the platform.

All the postcards being sold seemed to be adorned with flowers whilst all the stations displayed a giant portrait of the founder of the Soviet Union, Lenin.

Leo was something of a cheeky charmer so somehow he seemed to make friends with many of the locals. Once it was a couple of plump, middle-aged ladies who couldn't understand a word of what he said but nevertheless laughed at his jokes. On another occasion I got down off the train to see Leo walking back in my direction accompanied by a large strong looking young Russian man. Leo introduced

Leo being chatted up by two local ladies

him to me. As I cannot recollect his name I will call him Ivan. Before we separated Ivan insisted that we join him for dinner in the restaurant car and we indicated that we would be honoured to do so.

When we met up with Ivan at the restaurant we sat down at a table on the right-hand side of the car. Unusually the manager of the restaurant came to take our order rather than the waiter. While I watched the verbal intercourse between him and Ivan I thought the manager did not seem a happy soul, and got less happy when Ivan ordered a bottle of wine and three glasses. Despite the poor start we enjoyed the food and the wine and Ivan's company, so much so that Ivan asked for another bottle of wine. When this happened the manager and Ivan seemed to have angry words. I was puzzled as none of us were inebriated or behaving badly.

Eventually the meal came to an end and Ivan paid the bill and excused himself, indicating that he was going to his cabin. Shortly afterwards Leo said he would also return to his cabin but I hesitated because I had noticed the manager sitting writing something at his table. At one point he talked to a waiter and indicated with a nod of his head towards our table. When he had finished writing he asked the waiter to countersign the document. All the time I watched this as inconspicuously as possible as I sipped my drink.

Ivan was travelling on the train as far as Irkutsk, as were we, so Leo and I had told him that we wanted to return the compliment by inviting him for dinner with us again the next day. On the following morning, however, I was standing in the corridor looking out of the window when Ivan walked behind me. He had passed me before I could greet him but not before I noticed a look on his face that could only be described as angry. That night he didn't turn up for dinner and in fact we never saw him again. It seemed obvious to me that he had been told to get off the train, why and for what reason it was hard to think. Was it wrong to be too friendly to two foreigners? Quite possibly because we were to have other similar strange experiences before we left the Soviet Union.

14

The Paris of Siberia

Paris the incomparable.
Frederick Edwin Smith

When planning our journey Leo and I had decided to stop for a few days at a large city in the middle of the Soviet Union called Irkutsk which had been given the description "the Paris of Siberia". Before we reached Irkutsk, however, we passed an enormous lake called Lake Baikal—a mere 400 miles long, 40 miles wide and 1,500 metres deep. It is so big it is said to contain 20% of the world's freshwater fish!

Some 40 miles past Lake Baikal the train slowed and approached Irkutsk. As I got down from the train I was greeted immediately by a young woman saying "Mr Harry?". She introduced herself to Leo and I as "Thalia, I am your Intourist Guide whilst you are in Irkutsk". She was an attractive young woman who later told us she was studying languages at the University of Irkutsk. Working as a guide therefore gave her an opportunity to practice English with English-speaking foreigners.

Thalia escorted us and our luggage to a waiting taxi where she instructed the driver to take us to our hotel, its name I have forgotten. Whilst in the taxi Thalia explained that she was at our disposal for the whole period of our stay in Irkutsk. At the time our view of the Soviet Union was as an atheistic society, so rather provocatively we asked if we could visit a Russian Orthodox Church in the afternoon. She said that would be possible and having seen us into our hotel agreed to return later.

Our hotel was certainly no Ritz being very plain and box-shaped. We were directed to our room which was on an upper floor. When we reached that floor we found it bare of decoration, nothing except for a table at one end of the floor behind which sat a large unattractive woman. Apart from showing us to our room we have no idea what her function was (except perhaps to monitor those coming in and going out...).

The room itself was simple but comfortable. Then I discovered that I had an emergency. Most days in Australia I had plenty of exercise: swimming, tennis, squash etc. Sitting on a train for three solid days led to constipation

Thalia showing yours truly around Irkutsk

for me, and suddenly getting off and walking a bit suddenly reactivated the system. I told Leo to keep clear as I entered the bathroom for ten minutes. The relief was immense.

Thalia arrived with another taxi at the agreed time and we were taken to a very large and beautiful church where we were introduced to a young priest with a large black beard who reminded us very much of Rasputin. Afterwards Thalia asked what else we would like to do and after some discussion we asked to be taken to where the young people gathered. This turned out to be a beautiful park with a river running alongside it. We had enjoyed Thalia's company that day but we told her that the next day we would like to wander the city on our own and would see her next when she came to collect us to take us back to the station on the day after that.

The next day what we wanted to do first was a sad task because we had to say farewell to our new friend Yuji who was leaving Irkutsk one day before us. Yuji was delighted when we told him we would like to come and bid him farewell. However when we asked his Intourist Guide if we could accompany her and Yuri to the station all she said was it was "not necessary". We explained that we knew it was not necessary but we wanted to do it anyway because Yuji

With Yuji in Irkutsk

was our friend. She repeated it was not necessary. Although we persisted, she kept saying the same thing. Realising we were wasting our time with this guide we whispered to Yuji "don't worry, we will be there!"

The next morning Leo and I set off to walk to the station. It was a good walk but not difficult. We soon found Yuji who was delighted to see us. His guide lady looked a bit grim though!

We were still to have yet another disconcerting experience in Irkutsk however. As we tried to get back to our hotel we asked for help from a young man who was carrying a large musical instrument in a case. Not only did he tell us which way to go, but he also said that he would escort us there.

As we walked we exchanged information about ourselves and he was obviously impressed by our travels. When we got to our hotel, we invited him up to our room to continue our discussions. He seemed happy about this especially when we showed him photos. It was nearly time for the evening meal so we asked him to accompany us to the Hotel Dining Room where we would buy him dinner. He seemed very happy to be invited so we set off. Then things got very strange. As we entered the hotel dining room our friend very suddenly said he had better not join us and perhaps should go. Although we asked him to reconsider, he said he couldn't. We thanked him for his help and wished him well as he walked away. What was behind this change of mind? I think paranoia struck deep in the Soviet Union (and still does today).

The next day Thalia came to our hotel to take us to the station. Whilst we were waiting for the train to arrive, Leo took a walk and I chatted with Thalia. She said that she hoped that her proficiency in languages would result in a job that took her overseas, perhaps as a translator, even, who knows, as a diplomat. I wished her well. Leo returned and the train arrived, we hoisted our luggage onto the train, waved goodbye to Thalia and Irkutsk and set off on the 5,191-kilometre journey to Moscow.

15

Moscow Here We Come!

> *Be not afraid of every stranger,*
> *start not aside at every danger.*
> George Peele

As the Trans-Siberian train left Irkutsk we still had an immense distance to travel to get to Moscow. Leo and I found ourselves in different cabins again, nothing new there! I found myself sharing a cabin with a Russian family: father, mother and two children. They seemed shy, if not uneasy with my presence, and for the first day we greeted each other with polite smiles only, because of course we couldn't speak a common language.

The train continued to stop at least four times a day. What broke the ice between us happened following one of those stops when the family returned with lots of food purchased on the platform. As the train moved off again they sat down around the table, unpacked all the boxes, and started to eat. They had not been eating for long though before the father turned to me and signalled that I was welcome to join them. I expressed my appreciation and joined them at their meal.

We began to converse as best we could and I began to understand that they were asking me where I came from and where I was going to. At first I mentioned the names of countries: England, Australia, Japan, etc. I held out my arms, thinking they might understand that I had flown from Australia to Japan. Despite my game of charades they were still confused so I got out some paper and started to draw a rough, but hopefully recognizable, map of the world. I added planes and ships and trains to the map. Some understanding was achieved however and the father communicated his understanding to his wife and children, though they remained astonished probably because at that time Soviet citizens couldn't travel freely outside the Soviet Union unless they were diplomats.

After that our relationship was far more relaxed, even friendly, and it helped when I brought back ice cream from the platform to share with them. However, they were not travelling all the way to Moscow so after a couple of days we said farewell to each other and I continued on to Moscow with the carriage all to myself.

St Basil's Cathedral

Nine or ten days after boarding the Trans-Siberian at Khabarovsk (I'd lost count) the train eventually arrived at Moscow. Officious Intourist people arranged for our transit by taxi to our hotel, The Hotel Metropole. We found this hotel was close to The Red Square and also if we looked out of our windows and to the right we could see the theatre housing the world-famous Bolshoi Ballet.

MOSCOW HERE WE COME!

As we had only a few days in Moscow we unpacked, checked our room for bugging equipment, and then went off to see the Red Square. The beautiful St Basil's Cathedral was at one end of the square. The building of this cathedral was commissioned by the Tsar Ivan the Terrible and it is said that he was so pleased with the beauty of the building that when it was finished he put out the eyes of the architect responsible so that he wouldn't be able to build any other building to surpass it. I can think of better rewards and today's architects must be grateful that they were not around then!

The queue to see Lenin's tomb

The walls of the Kremlin lay along one long side of the square and in front of them there was a long line of people queuing up to see the tomb holding the embalmed body of Vladimir Ilyich Lenin, the founder of the Soviet Union. Fortunately for us two, however, we didn't have to join this long queue because there was a smaller queue intended especially for foreign visitors to use (they probably didn't want to keep us away long from spending!). We joined the queue, followed it into the tomb and around the body of Lenin, before moving out once more into the fresh air.

After Lenin's tomb we went to see what the shopping experience was like at the GUM Department Store which bordered the Red Square opposite the Kremlin. The purchasing procedure turned out to be somewhat complicated: you find what it is that you want to buy and check its price, you then go to a cashier where you pay for it and obtain a receipt, after which you return to where your purchase is and present the receipt of payment before finally take possession. And the consumer choice in Soviet Russia? Nichego (zilch)..

Leo and I were celebrating our respective birthdays whilst in Moscow so we had asked all our friends and relatives to send us birthday cards and to direct them to the British Embassy to see if they reached there safely. So on the next day we walked over the Moskvoretsky Bridge to visit the Embassy on the other side of the Moskva River. We received a shock when we went to move through the large gates of the Embassy as a Russian guard moved to block our way. Somehow we explained our purpose and we were let in. A young diplomat came to meet us and arranged for a cup of tea whilst our mail was collected. When our mail arrived there was so much that it was obvious that most of it had got through ok. Leo and I were to have much pleasure in reading the comments of everyone.

Our few days in Moscow soon passed and it was time to travel the final leg of our journey to England. We caught our next train which was to take us out of the Soviet Union and into Poland. Unfortunately before we could leave the Soviet Union we had to meet Soviet Customs people at the border. One male and one female entered the carriage that Leo and I shared with others. Leo's luggage got a cursory look before the lady turned to me and asked me to identify my luggage. I pointed out the four bags that were mine. Then just as had happened when I entered the Soviet Union I was asked to open all of it! I had to get it down from the racks and open the cases one by one. When the lady failed to find any State property that I was leaving the country with she finally, with perhaps some disappointment, left me to put it all back again. She then left the carriage without a thank you or a smile.

When the train moved off again we not only exited the Soviet Union but **we had completed a rail journey that had traversed the whole of the Asia continent!**

16

Coming Home

Seek home for rest, for home is best.
Thomas Tusser

Leaving the Soviet Union the train moved into Poland—still behind the Iron Curtain but where the views from the train were far more relaxing. Teenagers cycled along the paths bordering the railway line and on one occasion we even saw a young woman dressed in only a bikini riding a horse!

On arrival in Warsaw a taxi took us to the Hotel Bristol (with that name I was beginning to feel almost in England already!). We were to stop in the Polish capital for only one night so we quickly freshened up and went out to see the sights. Apart from the immense Palace Of Culture And Science we also discovered the old city where the young and old gathered for drinks or meals. The girls were eye-catching too dressed in mini skirts, the fashion of the 1960s.

The acquaintance was to be very short because the next day we joined the train that was to take us on to East Germany. At this time of course post-war Germany was split into two, one part called East Germany ruled by the Soviet Union, the other part called West Germany administered by the so-called Western Powers of the United States, Great Britain and France.

We were all trying to get some sleep when the train entered East Germany, only to be woken by East German Customs officials opening the doors to our carriages and yelling "Passports". Apart from that there were no apologies for waking us, no smiles, only a look at the passport photo followed by a stare at our tired faces. However, this was not to be the only time we were disturbed because the whole thing was to be repeated when we drew back the Iron Curtain and entered West Germany.

As the train moved on through West Germany and later through Belgium I got excited by my imminent homecoming and I often leaned out of the train window to look up the train in the direction of England. Unbeknown to me this was later going to have an adverse effect on my eyes.

Eventually the train arrived at Ostend in Belgium

which meant that **we had completed a transit of the European continent!**

After boarding the ferry taking us to Dover in England I told Leo that I was going to go to the front of the boat to see the White Cliffs Of Dover come into view as this was supposed to be a very emotional experience for Englishmen to see after a long sojourn overseas. A wind was blowing from England as I stood and savoured this experience!

17

Home Sweet Home

When as a child I laughed and wept,
Time crept; ... When I became a full-grown man,
Time ran.
Canon Henry Twells

The journey across the Channel was short so it was not long before my feet were back on English soil again, the first time in over nine years.

In Dover I was only hours away from my family, but I suddenly found that I had a big problem—my eyes were in terrible shape. They had become so bloodshot through looking into the wind from first the trains and then from the ferry that suddenly I could hardly see out of them!! My eye condition was so bad that I felt that I couldn't return home to my family looking so stressed. So despite haven't finished a journey all round the World amazingly I felt that I would have to delay my arrival in Luton. But where would we stop!

HOME SWEET HOME

Fortunately help was at hand! On the train and boat Leo and I had made friends with a young lady called Helen who was travelling home from Greece where she had been working as a teacher for two years. And luck was on our side because she lived with her mother in St Albans which was only ten miles from Luton. Helen suggested that we spend the night in St Albans where we could be fed, washed and rested whilst my eyes recovered. She made a phone call from London to her mother and asked her if she could bring home two Aussie guys! Her mother appeared to give an unhesitant yes.

I was to suffer just one more misfortune before I got back to Luton, although I was not to find about it until I was back in Luton. What happened was that I had placed my jacket with my luggage in the overhead luggage racks of the train to London. What I didn't notice however was that sometime in the journey to London my passport fell from my jacket pocket and lodged itself somewhere out of sight. I had travelled all around the world only to lose my passport in England. Perhaps there was some good fortune in this anyway because life could have been complicated if I had lost the passport in the Soviet Union. As a consequence in the months ahead I had to get a temporary passport to use for my return to Oz, only to hear later that my lost passport had been found in England and was to be returned to me via Canberra.

Helen's mother collected us at St Albans Station and drove us to her home where we were made welcome, allowed to bath, change into fresh clothes, and finally fed with a great meal. In the morning I was taken to a pharmacy to get some medicine for the eyes. This had some therapeutic effect so I said perhaps I should make a move to get to Luton. Mrs Jones insisted on driving us there. Shortly after therefore I was seeing Pomfret Avenue for the first time in nearly a decade. I had a shock. When I left in 1961 the road was almost empty of cars but by 1970 cars were lined up on both sides of the road and parked one behind each other for the whole length of the street.

The car stopped outside Number 57 and I climbed the steps and knocked the front door. As I stood there I heard my mother call out "that must be the telegram Mike said he would send" (which I hadn't been able to because I had been told on the ferry that the telegram service was unavailable on the day that I needed it!).

When Mum opened the door, she discovered me and yelled "it's Mike" before holding me and giving me the first kiss for such a long time. In very short time Dad was there and I got a second embrace.

HOME SWEET HOME

Back with Mum and Dad

Suddenly Mum remembered I was not supposed to be alone and said "Where's Leo? Leo came up the steps and received embraces of his own. I then introduced my parents to Helen and her mother and Mum asked them in true English fashion to come in for a tea. They were such considerate people however that they gracefully declined because they feared they would be intruding. Leo and I thanked them profusely and waved them as they began their return to St Albans. Later that day I was reunited with my sister Christine.

In the days that followed my sister Sylvia came to Luton with her husband Atam and their 21 month old son Justin,

Leo being slapped (or was it patted?) by Mike's mum

and then shortly afterwards my brother Raymond, his wife Jean, and their three kids: Lesley, Angela and Stephen. On the 4th of July there was a welcome home party with 130 relatives and friends invited. Leo and I were invited over the next 13 weeks to visit many of these good folks all over the country. One of the consequences of all this hospitality (remember the parable of The Prodigal Son!!) was a surge in my weight. I had left Oz weighing 11 stone. I had lost 6 pounds travelling across the World arriving in England weighing 10 stone 8 pound only to leave England some two months later weighing 12 stone!! I have never seen the underside of 12 stone since.

Nevertheless time passed all too quickly. Apart from the visits to relatives and friends I also made a trip to Edinburgh to see the Commonwealth Games. I got used too to having the family around so leaving them again was not going to be easy, for them or for me!

18
Return to Oz

If you want to go quickly, go alone.
If you want to go far, go together.
African proverb

Our last week in England came around all too quick and we were flying back to Australia on the Thursday.

On the Monday morning although I am known to be a very early riser I decided for some reason to lie-in. As I lay there I heard the doorbell ring and my mother go to answer it. I wondered who was calling so early. Mum opened the front door and I heard the lady there say "Good morning, are you Mrs Doris Harry". My bedroom was just above the front door and I could hear quite clearly that the lady was a Salvation Army officer. My mother was a little bit concerned to find them there as this was a rare occurrence. After a short time she was told that her brother Albert had died, "gone to glory" was the way his death was announced. After the officers left, I came downstairs and hugged mother who was of course in tears. Albert was the first of her eight siblings to die and now his funeral was going to be on Friday, the day after I left for Oz.

Thursday arrived, and Leo and I were driven to Heathrow by dad. Mum came as did Chris, Sylvia, Atam, Justin, Aunt Freda (Mum's sister) and her husband Charlie. Leo and I were also happy to see Megan there, come to say au revoir to us. Naturally it was a difficult farewell as there was to be a funeral the next day and I had to reassure everybody that they wouldn't have to wait so long this time to see me again.

The journey back to Oz was not going to be easy however as we were travelling at the beginning of the period when the Palestine Liberation Organisation were hijacking planes and threatening to blow them up with all the passengers on board if the Western Powers did not agree to the PLO's demands. There was a consequence to this for us because whenever the plane stopped anywhere passengers were not allowed to disembark to a transit lounge. After London the plane stopped at Rome, Tehran and New Delhi and Leo and I had to remain aboard while the plane refuelled, boarded new passengers etc. Because the air conditioning didn't work unless the plane was flying, the inside

Leo in rickshaw in Hong Kong

of the plane became very hot and uncomfortable especially at New Delhi where we watched the heat shimmer outside.

After being inside the plane for a full 20 hours the plane eventually landed at Hong Kong. We had seen this fabulous city on the flight to Japan months earlier but on this occasion we were able to get off and look around for a couple of days. We found the city not only to be noisy and active during the day but never quiet even at night.

Finally however it was time to move on and our next plane journey took us to the city of Darwin in the Northern territory of Oz. After a brief stop there we took off on the final leg of the journey to our homes in Sydney. We saw this beautiful city from the air, it was Sunday afternoon, and we were due to start work the next morning! **I had travelled half way round the world by air!**

19
Decision Time

Our course is clear, our decisions made.
Franklin Delano Roosevelt

When I left my Sydney office back in June I had been working on a Census. However this had finished during the time I was away so I found myself being referred to new work as a team leader in the Building And Construction Branch.

I sat side by side with another team leader, Phil Norris, and in front of us in straight lines were our respective teams. I had four in my team one of whom was an extrovert lass called Rosa Melino. Rosa had been born in Italy but had come with her family to Australia when she was aged five. She was a brave girl however, because she had decided to leave her home town of Ballina, some 500 miles north of Sydney, to come to the big smoke to get new work.

DECISION TIME

Perhaps because she was of Italian origin her mood could alternate from high to low. Phil and I always wondered what each new day would bring when she arrived. If she was in a good mood she would give us a beaming smile and wave to us from the entrance of the office. On the other hand, if she was in a bad mood (perhaps her boyfriend had upset her the previous night) then she wouldn't smile or wave but would walk down the aisle to her desk without making a single greeting. On such occasions Phil and I resorted to banter such as "has Rosa come in, Mike" to which I would reply "No, she couldn't have, Phil, I would have heard her". After a while she couldn't stop laughing and we were able to revive her spirits.

Arriving back in Oz I had no accommodation of my own but I was able to stop with my friends Peter and Sally Parsons for a month during which period I found myself a small flatlet in St Leonards.

It was time to make a big decision. When I had left Oz in June I knew that when I returned to Oz later in the year I would have to decide whether to stay in Australia or whether to return to the UK.

On the leave side I had come to Australia at the young age of 19 not necessarily to make a home there. I had made that great sea journey in 1961 because I wanted an adventure and I had developed an addiction to travel. There were two major impacts that might lead to a decision to leave.

The first of these was the great family I had in the old country and I especially missed them now having just spent time with them again. The second was the lure of Europe. Although I had just taken the long train journey which took me through Poland and the Germanys, there were still so many other fascinating countries in Europe that I had yet to see.

Conversely, what pressures were there to stay? First among these I loved the country of Australia which was such a fascinating land, absolutely unique in fact. I also loved the sunshine, the heat, and the beaches. I had a good job at the Bureau which I enjoyed. Then, perhaps pre-eminently, there were the great friends I had. If I left I would miss all of these and furthermore have to find a new job when I got to England.

Some things were not problems. Although I had thought about buying a property, and saved to that end, I had not made the first step. Also although I had had a close relationship with at least two young ladies I was not engaged or married.

It was a very difficult decision to make but in the end I

made the decision to leave. For the time being I told no-one of what I had planned. I was going to tell my family after I had made the travel bookings and could give them a date of arrival.

In January I finally told my friends Leo, Laurie, Peter and Sally but asked them to keep it to themselves. I would tell all my other friends after I had given the Bureau my notice of leaving.

It was just after I had made that decision to leave that life became amusing. It was then that Rosa told me of her plans for the coming year. It seemed she planned to travel to Italy to see the land and region of her birth. She delighted in her attempts to make me jealous by telling me all the pleasures that Italy offered. "Wouldn't it be wonderful if we could meet there" she said. "Wouldn't it" I replied and went on to say "if we did then I can suggest where we could meet". "Where" she asked. "The Arch De Constantine" I replied". "If only boss" she sighed.

The next decision was important but not so hard, that is how would I travel home. I could of course fly home but I quickly discounted that option as flying can be so boring and there was half a World en route to see. Consequently, I decided to book myself a passage on a ship called the *Fairstar*, which was the sister ship to the Sitmar Line's

Fairsky that had brought me to Oz some ten years earlier. The ship was scheduled to leave Pyrmont on Thursday the 27th of May and sail to England via the Pacific and Atlantic Oceans. I was delighted to learn that I would be leaving Sydney three days before Rosa was due to leave. How that would annoy her!

It was of course an exciting time but suddenly there was some really bad news. It came in a strange way. I was hauling a cabin trunk back from the city one evening and had got to the front door of my flat. As I got my keys out to open the door I could see a letter waiting for me in the middle of the porch and somewhat eerily the moonlight was shining right onto it. I had a premonition the news would not be good, and I was right.

Getting inside the house I picked up the letter, saw it was from my sister Sylvia, and sat down to read it with a heavy heart. Since I had left England my mother, father and sister Chris had moved from Luton to Polperro, a coastal village in my father's birth county of Cornwall. One night my sister Chris had gone out for the evening with my niece Lesley and two local boys. Later, as they were about to return home, the driver let two other young people join them in the car. The worst happened. As the car was driven through the Cornish winding lanes, the driver went too fast

DECISION TIME

on one of the bends and the car turned over. The tragic result was the death of the driver and injuries to all the others. Chris and Lesley sustained the worst of the injuries and Sylvia's letter informed me that they were both in Plymouth Hospital with terrible back injuries.

Sylvia said that they were both in a lot of pain and suggested it would help if I wrote a letter. All former plans for the evening were immediately put on hold as I wrote that letter. I decided that it might provide some cheer if I told them of my plans to return home.

Although the injuries sustained by Chris and Lesley were to their backs and have had long-term repercussions for both girls they have both moved on with bravery and determination.

20

Au Revoir Australia

*It is much easier to begin
than to finish.*
Plautus

The months passed quickly and I regularly asked myself whether I was doing the right thing leaving Oz. I loved Australia and had a great bunch of friends there. There were going to be great compensations though. First of these was I would be crossing two great oceans, first the Pacific, then the Atlantic. When I eventually got back to England I would then be reunited with my family and I would also be able to see more of the country of my birth. Finally of course there was the opportunity to see more of the varied countries of Europe. I became reconciled to changing a new world for the old country.

Sometime in April I gave notice at the Bureau and at the same time let all my friends know of my imminent departure. My friends were very surprised because they had grown used to my presence.

Then of course I had to break the news to Rosa whose reaction was to scream "Michael Harry, this cannot be true!!". I assured her that it was and suggested that after all it might be possible for the two of us to meet at the *Arch De Constantine* the next year.

The remaining month was a time for many farewells. My boss told me that he was very disappointed that I was going because I had done such a good job restoring order to a Section that had been so chaotic before I took it over. My tennis friends held a farewell picnic at a beautiful spot

Farewell barbeque by Sydney Harbour

overlooking the harbour, an occasion that really brought it home to me what I was going to miss.

Then it was time for Rosa to leave. Originally I was going to be leaving before her but in the meantime the sailing date of one of our ships had been altered so that in the end she was after all leaving two days before me. There is a photograph of Phil Norris and I with Rosa and her friends and family on her ship the *Achille Lauro* (the same liner that was to be in the world's headlines following its hijack in 1985 by the PLO).

The *Fairstar*

AU REVOIR AUSTRALIA

Next it was my turn to go. In the day that followed I got most of my luggage down to the *Fairstar* with the help of a work colleague, Alan Kelley. Finally it was departure day and Leo took me and my cabin luggage to the ship before we went off to Chinatown for a feast with my friends to drown their sorrows (or was it to celebrate my departure?).

After the feast I was taken back to the Harbour to board the *Fairstar*. A photo shows a hardcore of mates on the quayside to make sure that I didn't change my mind and get off the boat. Those seven were Leo Detsikas, Leo's brother John, Phil Norris, Laurie Coleman, Dennis Hale, Alan Kelley and Brian Davoren.

Crowds cheering my departure

At midnight the sirens went and the *Fairstar* moved slowly and steadily away from the Quay. My friends cheered my departure. We passed the Heads in darkness and sailed in the direction of the Tasman Sea. The sea voyage around the world had begun.

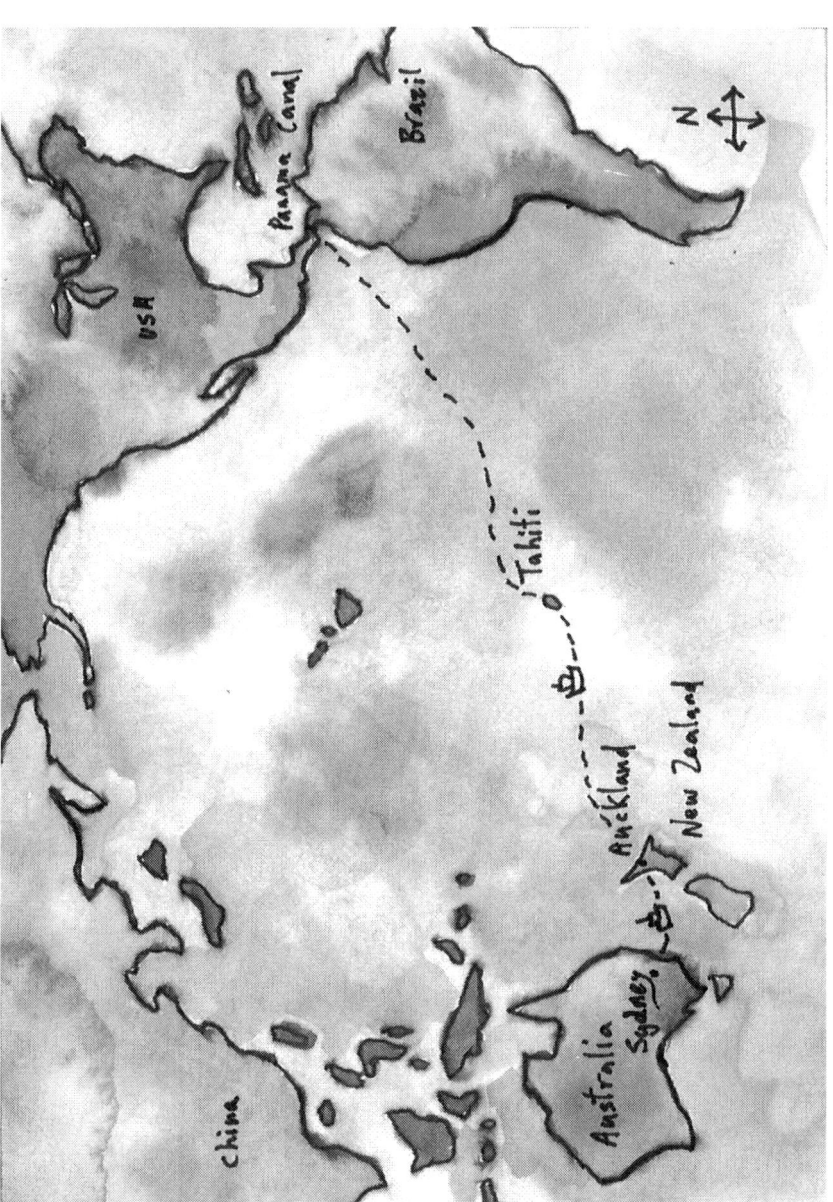

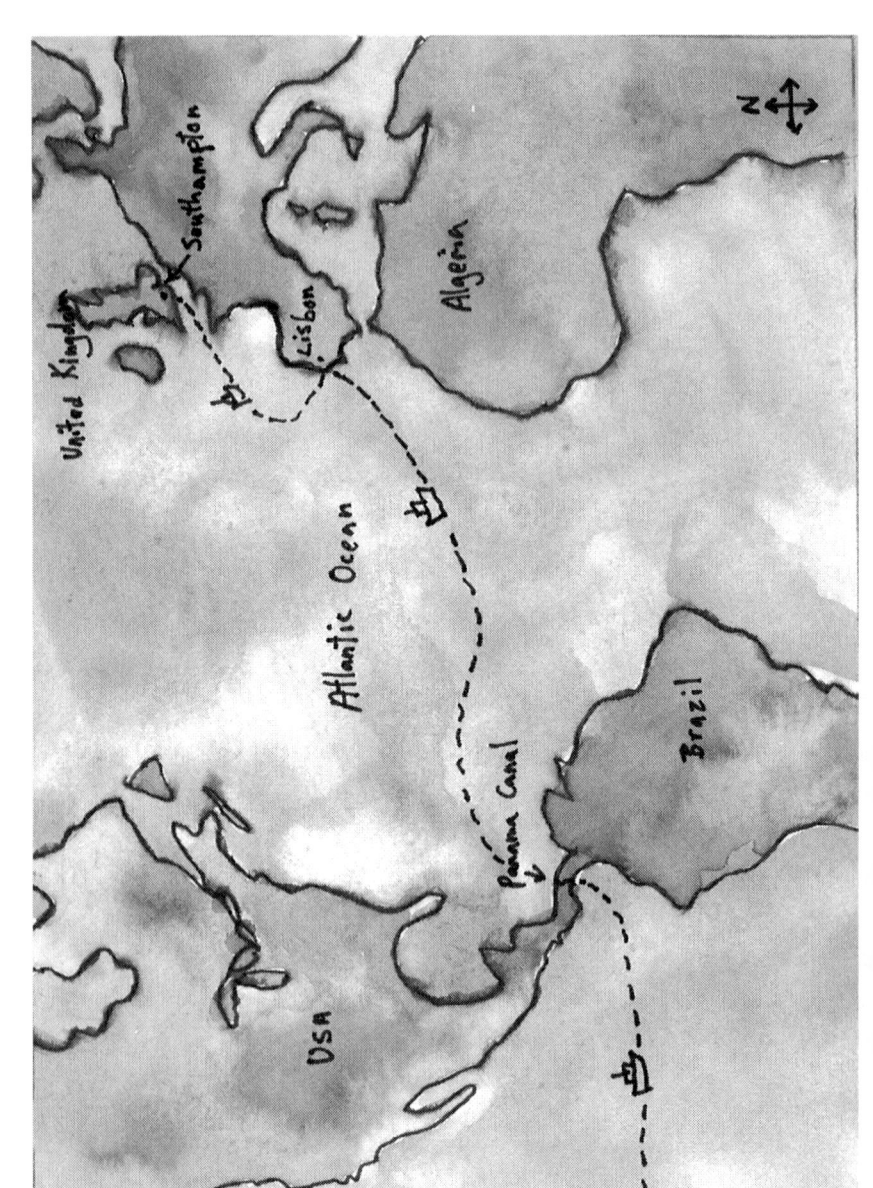

21

Crossing the Pacific and the Atlantic

The broad blue sky above thee spread.
The boundless ocean round thee.
Revd Henry Lyte

As the *Fairstar* sailed out of the harbour my emotions were very mixed. On one side I was sad to be leaving beautiful Sydney and the great friends I had made there. On the other side my departure produced other excitements. Immediately there was the excitement of getting to know some of my fellow passengers. Then there was the thought that at the end of the journey I would be united again with my family. And finally there was the wonderful prospect of the journey itself, first to New Zealand, then across the Pacific Ocean, the biggest ocean in the world, then through the Panama Canal, across yet another ocean, the Atlantic Ocean, before making land in Europe, first at Portugal before finally arriving at Southampton.

There was a time, after leaving Sydney Harbour behind, that I along with many others made our way to our respective cabins to sleep. However just as on previous journeys at sea, my cabin was very low down in the boat. When I reached it I found that I had one cabin mate, a fellow called Ray. Apparently Ray hadn't taken to Australia in the same way that I had, one of the reasons he explained was that he missed the warm beer of the north of England! Like me, he had been an assisted migrant so he was required to stop in Australia for at least two years before he could leave. If he left before the two years were up then he would be required to refund the Australian Government the cost of his fare to Australia. As a consequence he was leaving Australia two years plus one day after he arrived!! Me? I enjoyed cold Fosters Lager.

The distance from Sydney to Auckland was 1,340 miles (2,155 km) and it took the ship about three days to sail this distance. I think the sea was very rough because I do remember having great difficulty sleeping. Eventually, however, we arrived at Auckland and the passengers were informed that they had about 12 hours to see the city. I joined others to walk into town. I remember that there was

CROSSING THE PACIFIC AND THE ATLANTIC

a long hill to climb away from the Port, after that I recalled nothing because I felt so tired. Three nights without sleep had caught up with me so I excused myself from those I was with and made my way back to the boat. Reaching it, I lay down on my bunk and soon went to sleep. The next that I remember is waking up some over twelve hours later when the *Fairstar* was way out at sea and I had just had probably the longest sleep of my life.

One good discovery about the journey that I was on was that it was being shared with a lot of young ladies. Apparently the custom at that time was, when the young ladies had finished college, they took a year out to go overseas, mainly to the UK where they would hire a van and go travelling in Europe. A good friend of mine from Sydney had arranged introductions for me to two attractive working colleagues of his—shall call them Jane and Jill. When the *Fairstar* had left NZ waters it had been decided that there should be a "Get-Together" Ball because after Auckland all the folks who were travelling to the UK were now on board. I partnered Jane and my cabin mate Ray partnered Jill.

The Ball did not go according to plan. On the night of the ball we four went to the large hall where the Ball was to be. A small band was there playing some welcoming music but apart from them there were probably no more

With three young ladies on the Fairstar

than a dozen other persons. The reason for this was that the ship was suddenly travelling through very bad weather that was causing the sea to be very, very rough. I think we four got ourselves a table and ordered drinks and at some point tried to dance. The trouble was though, one moment you were dancing over on the right of the ballroom, then a moment later you found yourself propelled to the other side of the ballroom. This could not go on, especially when our two young ladies began to feel ill. Ray and I set off to accompany them to their cabins. I managed to get Jane down two floors to the point where we had to cross a foyer to enter a corridor on the other side where her cabin could be found. I had been supporting her all the way from the

CROSSING THE PACIFIC AND THE ATLANTIC

ballroom and I kept hold of her as we crossed the foyer. Unfortunately poor Jane was unable to enter the corridor without first being sick in the receptacle over there. When this was all over I helped Jane the last few yards to her cabin. At the door she thanked me and assured me that she would be ok, so I wished her goodnight and went to have my whisky at the bar. Later I was to find out that it was in these very same seas that the boat of Sir Francis Chichester, on his record-making first single-handed sail around the world, had turned over (somehow he managed to right it!).

As the *Fairstar* moved on, the seas became much calmer, even placid. It was then that we were able to see the exciting sight of very large fish accompanying the ship. Also the beautiful vision of the ocean spreading out vast distances in all directions!! During this period I got to know many other voyagers. Among them was a lovely young lady called Julie who was going to further her musical career in England. Also there were two sisters from Queensland called Val and Marie and a lassie called Lyn who went on to marry a guy in our group called Barrie.

Days turned to weeks until eventually we reached our second stop, the beautiful island of Tahiti. When you arrived at Tahiti you really felt you were travelling because these islands were not the usual place for a holiday. Apart

Tahiti

for being known for their charm, the main reasons we have heard of the islands were because Captain Cook took his ship there to observe a solar eclipse, and later on Captain Bligh brought his ship the *Bounty* there. The latter visit of course was followed by the infamous Mutiny.

During our short stay on Tahiti I remember eating delicious food and watching Tahitian ladies doing their local dancing. It was not long however, before we were called back to the *Fairstar* to sail on to the Panama Canal.

Some ten years before in 1961 when I was sailing to Australia my ship the *Fairsky* had sailed through the Suez Canal to transit from the Mediterranean Sea into the

CROSSING THE PACIFIC AND THE ATLANTIC

The Panama Canal

Indian Ocean, now I was on the other side of the World in another great canal moving from the Pacific Ocean into the Atlantic Ocean. It was an amazing experience to move from lock to lock through the canal. Soon after entering each lock, the lock was filled with loads of water thus raising the ship. The ship was eventually allowed to sail on before entering another lock where the same thing happened again. In all the ship was raised an amazing 85 feet. On the Atlantic side the reverse was done to lower the ship down to sea level on that side. During this transit we were allowed off the ship for tours of Panama City and Balboa before completing our exit from the canal.

After leaving the canal our next port of call was originally intended to be Curacao but unfortunately this was not to happen as we were told that there were political disturbances there. As a consequence we left the Panama Canal behind and the *Fairstar* began the long sail across the Atlantic.

As we sailed the Atlantic I continued to read two books, one was *The Coming War Between China And Russia*, by Harrison Salisbury, and the other was the best-selling escape book *Papillon* which had been a gift from my former colleagues back in Sydney. The rest of the time was spent in the bachelor's paradise that was the *Fairstar*.

As we moved north all we passengers tried to imagine our future landing when we would eventually arrive at Southampton. Before we got there we were given the opportunity of one more stop, this time at Lisbon in Portugal. It was sunny and hot there and we enjoyed seeing some of the local sights. Eventually it was back to the *Fairstar* and the last sea journey to Southampton.

Back in 1961 I had sailed halfway round the world via the Indian Ocean to reach Australia. Now I had just completed sailing to the UK via the Pacific and Atlantic Oceans. **I had sailed all round the world!**

22

Welcome Back Mike!

*There are three kinds of lies: lies,
damned lies, and statistics.*
Disraeli

My father was waiting for me at Southampton along with (I think) my Uncle Charlie and family. I cannot recollect now whether we spent a short respite in my uncle's home in Petersfield or my father and I set off immediately to the new family home in Polperro, Cornwall.

Mum, Dad and Chris had left Luton and gone to live in Polperro during the previous Autumn. When we got there Mum was waiting for us but Chris was still in hospital, the result of that awful accident she had been involved in during the winter period. The next day I was taken to the hospital in Plymouth where Chris and our niece Lesley were still patients and still in plaster around the upper body. Despite this the spirits of the two girls were positive.

Browned off after long sea voyage

In the early weeks back in England in 1971 I not only met my brother and his family and my other sister Sylvia and her family but also travelled to Edinburgh to see the Edinburgh Festival. Whilst there I met up with some of my friends from the *Fairstar*.

After leaving Edinburgh I travelled by train to Plymouth Station where I was happy to meet not only my dad but also a young French couple called Milou and Genevieve. It seems that some years before Genevieve had come to Luton with her school and had been provided accommodation with my family. It was great fun having them in Cornwall with me and I was later to visit them in France.

Of course it was a time to get serious and find a job. At first I thought that I might find a job in Plymouth, which like Sydney was a city by the sea, so I contacted the local Employment Agency. My memories of the search though were that there was very little work available (could it really have been just two jobs, and one of those was as a fisherman!). As a consequence I decided that perhaps I should look for work in London.

My old friend Bernard (Bunny) Clarke offered me a room in his house in Luton whilst I found work. I attended a few interviews until I found and was offered a very interesting position as a Statistics Officer at an organisation called the Commonwealth Secretariat in a beautiful building near the Mall and St James Park. The Commonwealth Secretariat was like the civil service for the British Commonwealth and so I found myself working in a very large room with people from all over the Globe including India, Pakistan, Australia, Canada, New Zealand,

Nigeria, Kenya and many, many more. I was to work there for just over two years.

I now had a job, so the next thing was to find a place to live in London. Even this turned out not to be hard to achieve because I quickly found a comfortable bedsit in a lovely London suburb called East Putney.

In the months that were left in of that year I was to enjoy myself at work and at leisure, socialising with my work colleagues and my friends and family. I looked forward to holidaying in Europe in 1972.

Part II

The Decade of Europe – The 1970s

23

Back to Rome Again

All roads lead to Rome.
Proverb

One of the reasons that led to me making the decision to leave Oz was because of my desire to experience much more of Europe. When I left for Australia back in 1960, my only exposures to Europe had been the Olympic Games in Rome in 1960 and a long weekend in Paris in the spring of 1961. As I lived through my first English winter for over a decade, I began my plans to see once again the country that was, and still is, my favourite country to visit.

Sometime in the late Spring I set off by train heading for Rome, but on this occasion without making a stop in Paris en route. As we approached Italy the train stopped for a while in a long tunnel before finally emerging to be greeted by that (beautiful) Italian smell.

The last time I was in Rome I slept with two other

THE DECADE OF EUROPE – THE 1970S

young friends in a small tent; this time I lived in much more comfort in a very nice hotel called the Hotel Splendour.

The first thing I had to do the day after arriving in Rome was to meet up with Rosa. The reader will remember that Rosa was heading for Italy at almost exactly the same time that I was leaving Oz to return to England. Whilst Rosa was bursting with excitement because she would soon be in Italy, I had had to keep my plans secret from her until I handed in my notice. This didn't stop Rosa saying "wouldn't it be great if we could meet in Rome". I replied "Yes, I know where we should meet, it is the *Arch De Constantine*". In the end, however, we didn't meet at the Arch but in a restaurant. Afterwards Rosa took me around her city showing me the sights and talking non-stop. Amongst the highlights of the day were visiting the Protestant Cemetery and being introduced to espresso coffee at a point when my energy was low.

The day after meeting Rosa I set off from my hotel to see more of the city's delights. I had not been walking very long when I met another English guy also on his own whose name I cannot now remember so I will call him Phil. It was not long after we two had started walking together that we encountered a young woman who was looking as if she was lost so we stopped to see if we could help. She told us that she was in Rome for just one day and like us was out sightseeing. We invited her to join us, which she said she was happy to do. Her name was Villy and she was a very striking young woman. As she talked she told us that she was a glamour model and indeed after my return to London I found a magazine with her on the front cover. Of course this meant her figure was extremely striking and included a very large bosom. As a consequence during the day as we visited the Trevi Fountain, The Spanish Steps, and the Pensione, we found that we had to protect her from many of the local men who were constantly eyeing her up and moving closer to her.

During the evening we three stopped briefly in the gardens within my hotel after which Phil and I walked Villy safely back to her hotel. She had told us that she was catching the train in the morning so I said I would be happy to come to her hotel in the morning to assist her and her luggage to the station. She said she would appreciate that very much.

The next day I said my goodbyes to her at the station. We were to meet briefly later when she made a visit to London.

During the remaining few days I saw the Palace of Victor Emanuel and the Catacombs before getting the train back to England. My train journey home was enhanced by the company of two young guys who had been sailing a millionaire's yacht around Sicily. *Arrivaderci Roma*!

24

No Tulips in Amsterdam and Salad Days

*A Scotsman is never at home but
when he is abroad.*
Revd William Pitt Scargill

When I had arrived in Oz back in 1961 I soon discovered that potential employers there didn't recognize the GCE qualifications that I brought with me from England. Similarly when I arrived back in England in 1971, Civil Service Employers and others didn't recognize the Leaving Certificate and the Public Administration Diploma that I had brought back from Oz with me. Consequently I decided to enrol in a course called the Higher National Certificate in Business Studies to enhance my employability.

Whilst I was on this course I made friends with a

young Scottish guy called Graham Craik. I gained some notoriety with him and some of our fellow students when I suggested that we could use the half-hour interval between lessons to go for a quick pint at the local pub just opposite the college. This suggestion was greeted with enthusiasm and became a pleasant interlude.

During the end of term break in college in April 1974 Graham and I decided we would take a holiday in the Dutch city of Amsterdam. We were joined by another friend of Graham's called Bob.

We travelled to Amsterdam by catching a train from Liverpool Street followed by a ferry to the Hook of Holland where we boarded another train to Amsterdam. As we travelled we couldn't help but notice that the tulips that Holland was famous for seemed to have already been picked.

Amsterdam was delightful and the people not just friendly but able to speak perfect English. We were also amazed in Amsterdam to see the number of cyclists on the city roads, a much healthier atmosphere than the roads in London which were full of cars polluting the atmosphere. During our stay there we found there were a variety of restaurants that we could visit and so we were able to eat not only Dutch food but also Indonesian food, as well as Italian, Indian and Chinese.

NO TULIPS IN AMSTERDAM AND SALAD DAYS

There were many places to see there including the Rembrandt House, the Heineken Brewery, the Canals and of course the Redlight District but the most fascinating of all was The House Of Anne Frank where we were able to see the small rooms that she and her family were forced to live in for so long, right up until the time that they were discovered.

After we returned to London, Graham and I went back to college for the last term of our course. After two years of studying together the group we were in had become good friends so we decided to have a holiday together. Fortunately for us, one of our fellow students had an important position in the airline called JAL. At this time JAL was the airline for the country of Yugoslavia which was to break up after a civil war in 1991 thru 2001. Our friend, whose name I think was Peter Bulatovic, was able to arrange good value fares with his airline.

JAL airline had been given the unfortunate name of "Just about time" but on this occasion I think we got to Ljubljana (now Slovenia's capital city) in good time. From Ljubljana the group went by train to the port of Rijeka which is a seaside resort now in Croatia where we met up with Graham who was there with an Italian friend called Umberto (Huby for short).

THE DECADE OF EUROPE — THE 1970S

First thing we had to do was to find rooms to sleep in only to discover that most of the hotels were full. However, fortunately, we found a man limping in the street who was able to guide us to a place where five of us could stop. The next morning we met up with Graham and Huby and we all went to the beach.

At the beach I suddenly found that Graham couldn't swim so I started giving him lessons. After a short while he had learned how to float and he became so excited at being able to do this that he almost had an accident when a large boat came up behind him threatening to collide with him. Fortunately we were able to bring the upcoming boat to Graham's attention and so avoid the collision.

The next day Graham, Huby and I said farewell to the others and went to Pula to see the amphitheatre there. At night we had the use of Huby's small tent but as I had no sleeping bag it was decided that I should use the tent whilst the other two would sleep outside where they got bitten by mosquitos!!

The next day we three made our way to spend some time in Jesolo in Italy before Graham and I returning to Ljubljana for the flight home.

25

See Europe in 12 Days

*Italia! Oh Italia! Thou who hast the
fatal gift of beauty.*
Byron

In September 1975 I set out with a friend Ian Scott to travel to Brussels. We caught a train from Victoria to Dover where we boarded a boat sailing to Ostend. At Ostend we then caught a train to Brussels. We arrived there quite late but still managed to book into a hotel.

The next day we checked out the EEC headquarters in Brussels and enjoyed a good lunch that included Stella Artois beer, mussels and (a first for me) frogs legs. We then caught the train to Cologne (Koln) in Germany where we became somewhat concerned because we were told there were no privatzimmers or hotels available in Koln at all. Because of this we were given seats on a coach for a journey of 42km to Bad Honnef where we were able to get a relatively cheap room at the Hotel Bellevue, though the supper proved to be somewhat expensive. The next morning we enjoyed a good breakfast from a room that happily provided a good view overlooking the Rhine. After breakfast we were put in a coach back to Koln.

Then problems arose! In my case it was painful toothache—and this was at the beginning of a 12 day holiday! We somehow found a dentist for me who was able to stop the pain, but instructed me to get fillings done back in London. In Ian's case the problem was that he was leaving for London late that afternoon—he had only come for a weekend—and there was a problem with his flight. Fortunately he was able to get a solution to that and we were able to visit the magnificent Koln Cathedral together before we said our farewells. Whilst Ian went off to get his plane, I went to get an overnight train to Vienna (Wien) in Austria.

I stopped one night in Vienna before moving on to Graz and then to Zagreb in the country then known as Yugoslavia. From Zagreb I took a long, slow journey to Trieste in Italy. When I reached Trieste I phoned Umberto who I had met earlier in Rijeka. Huby instructed me to get a bus to his village which was called Godega.

When the bus reached Godega, Huby was there too

welcome me off the bus. Then life became strange after he invited me into the café nearby for a drink. Once inside there were two old gentlemen that Huby knew who apparently invited the two of us to play Bridge. I hadn't played for years but I agreed to play nevertheless and so we had this game where everything had to be interpreted for us by Huby. I cannot recollect who won.

After the café Huby took me back to his family home which was a magnificent place. Apparently his parents and his younger brother were away that weekend. In the afternoon we made some visits nearby and then went for a pizza in the evening. A little too much drink was consumed which led to a hangover. It didn't help when I woke up the next day with a sore head to hear Huby playing John Lennon's song "Imagine" very loudly on a piano.

One day later Huby and I set off by car to go to Padua where Huby had to enrol for University. During the day I saw the Padua Cathedral before meeting up with Huby in the evening. We went to a restaurant where we were joined shortly after by a friend of Huby called Franco who I was told was a film producer.

After a delicious meal Franco invited us to come and stop the night in his home and we set off in a bus to get there. After the journey out of the city we came to a very isolated area where we had to walk for a distance to Franco's home which turned out to be large house surrounded by a high wall. We went into what was perhaps "the lounge" but it was nothing like an English lounge, no carpet, no armchairs. Instead there were four chairs placed in a quadrangle around the room. Inset into the walls were rounded alcoves where busts etc were placed.

We three guys sat on the chairs having a few drinks and chatting for an hour or so before Franco thought perhaps we should be heading for bed. Franco then told me that I should have his bed which I said was not necessary. However, he insisted using the excuse that Huby and he had things to talk about. In the end I complied and went to his bedroom whilst Franco and Huby went to sleep in the adjoining room.

After reading a little I turned off the light and got ready to sleep. I could hear the two of them talking in the next room. After a while however a strange thing happened – I could hear the two of them talking but heard footsteps upstairs! The noise persisted whilst the other two kept talking in the adjoining room. Despite the very strange noise above my head I eventually went to sleep.

The next morning I woke to find that Franco had had to leave early for work so after breakfast Huby and I left to walk to the railway station where I was to get a train across North Italy. As we walked I told Huby about the footsteps upstairs and asked what had caused them. Huby then told me an extraordinary story. He claimed that the house we had just slept in had psychic phenomena. He said that he had probably been a guest in the house some 50 times without anything strange happening. Then, he said, one night Franco and he were sitting in the "lounge" room on two of the chairs when one of the other chairs in the room moved across the floor. He was shocked of course. He went on to say that they had also heard the noises the night before and further that this house was one of 200 houses in Italy that were being investigated by the Psychic Society of Italy. There had been many instances of poltergeist activity and Huby had witnessed one of them.

When I heard this my initial reaction was he was having me on, but he insisted that it was true. After some deliberation I decided that he was telling me the truth.

Eventually we reached the railway station and Huby saw me leave on the train to Milan.

I stopped for an overnight in Milan and remember being very impressed by the Duomo Cathedral there. In the evening I boarded the Mistral train to Paris.

In recent years I had got in touch with Shinako who

THE DECADE OF EUROPE — THE 1970S

I had first met on the ship that sailed from Japan to the Soviet Union. After arriving in the Soviet Union Shinako had accompanied us by train overnight to Khabarovsk but left us there to catch a plane to I think Norway where she was going to study music. Later I learned that she had moved from Scandinavia to come and live in Paris and had starting painting, what a talented girl! We had kept in touch so I phoned her and she insisted that I get out of the hotel that I was in and come and stop with her and her partner Ken who turned out to be a regular nice guy.

After a memorable time in Paris, with lots of reminiscences, I eventually said *adieu* to Shinako and Ken and caught a train from the Gare Du Nord back home to Victoria Station in London. The end of a great holiday, Europe in 12 Days or at least a good part of Europe, and some 2,416 miles!!

26

Mauritian Destiny & Destination South

In time comes she who God sends.
Proverb

The year 1975 was to be a very important one in my life. Although I was no longer working at the Commonwealth Secretariat I still returned there on Friday evenings to drink and socialise at the bar in Marlborough House. On one of those Fridays as I entered the property I saw an attractive young lady with her hair in a pigtail squatting down to admire the flowers in the bed beside the path. During that evening I learned that her name was Jeanine Li Kwong In and she was from an island in the Indian Ocean called Mauritius. Up until then my only knowledge of Mauritius was through my earlier enthusiasm for stamp

THE DECADE OF EUROPE – THE 1970S

collecting. That meeting became the start of a relationship that was to lead to marriage in 1980.

Fairly soon after we met, Jeanine decided to change her French name to her Chinese name of Fopin (which I understand translates to "Peace"!) Or Fo for short. I was to learn that she had many siblings, five were still in Mauritius, another one Peng was in England, Minchoo was in Hamburg, and two others, Yang and Nachin, were in the USA.

As a consequence of meeting Fo and discovering she had a sister, Minchoo, living in Hamburg I made a trip there by train in November 1975 and stopped with Minchoo and her husband Eugen. Hamburg is the second largest city in Germany with the second biggest port in Europe. Whilst there I visited Hannover before returning to London via Koln, Dortmund and Paris.

Come 1977 I decided to make another ambitious journey. It started with a train from Victoria to Dover then on to the Gare Du Nord in Paris. I stopped with Shinako and Ken for an overnight before boarding a train which took me all the way south through France to the town of Hendaye on the border with Spain where I changed trains to another that took me through the night to the Spanish capital of Madrid. The journey from Paris to Madrid was 1,458 km long and was the longest single rail journey that I had taken since the Trans-Siberian Railway back in 1970.

At the station I was able to book a room in Madrid at the Hotel Carrera. The next morning I went out early to look around Madrid and by midday I was feeling so hungry that I went into a restaurant to get a good lunch of the meal I understand was called paella. In the restaurant it seemed very strange because noon would be the beginning of lunchtime in London but in this Madrid restaurant I seemed to be the only customer. Although the staff were polite I had to wait a long time before food eventually arrived. I was to learn later that lunch in Spain tends to start at 13:30 and not 12:00! Also lunch time is two hours long instead of the one hour that it is in England and usually ends about 4:00ish! The evening meal starts approximately at 21:00!! In the afternoon I visited Madrid's Prado Museum to see its great art collection.

The next day I took a train to Barcelona in the northeast of Spain where I stopped overnight so that I could take in Las Ramblas and see the unique looking Sagrada Familia Cathedral.

I am sure that Barcelona has changed since but I was amused over my experience visiting a public toilet. I found myself being shown to a toilet by an old lady who unlocked the toilet door for me, then handed me a few sheets of toilet paper before finally putting out her hand to receive a gratuity!! This was the 1970s after all.

After a brief stay in Barcelona I caught the train again this time back into France, destination Nimes, where I was looking forward to meeting up with Genevieve and Milou Lauzel, the couple that I had met at my parent's home in Polperro back in 1971.

There was no food to be obtained on the train so I was forced to rely on the Barcelona breakfast to see me through to Nîmes. Another problem was that I needed to find an exchange to obtain French money (this must have been before I got my first credit card!).

Unfortunately on reaching Nîmes my fortunes were not about to revive. Some days back in Spain I had sent a postcard warning them of my imminent arrival, however when I rang the doorbell of the flat of Mr and Mrs Lauzel there was no response. I decided that they were both out shopping so I went away for a while returning twice but with the same result. I began to think that perhaps they were on holiday and thus had not seen my postcard. Feeling very disappointed I began to make plans to travel on to Strasbourg overnight as I didn't have any money to even buy myself a meal as all the banks and exchanges were now closed.

Then my luck changed! A couple I encountered at the front door to the block of flats where Genevieve's parents lived were able to tell me that the Lauzels would be back from work at 19:00. They soon arrived home, they had never seen the postcard, and it in fact did not turn up until a few days after I had left Nimes.

The welcome was wonderful however, Genevieve and Milou were informed that I had arrived and quickly joined us. I had barely eaten all day but the meal that evening was a delight! It began with some starters which I was unfamiliar with, but then continued to make a dinner of maybe seven courses. Great food and a wonderful welcome.

Over the next few days I was introduced to the lovely city that is Nîmes. There were some great markets, but also the Pont Du Gard which was an aqueduct that had been built by the Romans to bring water to Nimes. The aqueduct is the highest of all Roman aqueducts and was built in three tiers. I was invited by Milou and Genevieve to join them in a walk across the aqueduct and I was happy to concur. However I presumed that I would be walking through one of the enclosed tiers. Imagine my surprise when Milou and Genevieve set off to walk across the open top! There was no fence to stop you falling down hundreds of feet and to add to my concern there were rectangular holes in the path which were forcing you to walk closer to the edge. I followed them and was very happy to reach the other side.

Eventually however it was time to say au revoir to these wonderful folks and I was back on the train to Strasbourg. Strasbourg is in Alsace, France, but has a German name. I discovered that this city has been passed between French and German control since 1681 when it was conquered by French forces.

After a short stay in Strasbourg my journey took me briefly through Luxembourg, back through Paris and finally home to London. The total distance covered had been 4,857 km.

27
The Final Years of the 1970s

Fortune effects great changes in brief moments.
Proverb

In 1978 I made my last long journey of the 1970s. It started in November when I took the train from Liverpool Street to Harwich. From there I took a ferry to the Hook Of Holland. Trains followed to Hengelo on the Dutch border and then into Germany to Hamburg where I stayed once more with my sister-in-law Minchoo, her husband Eugen, and their lovely daughters.

Leaving Hamburg after a few days I travelled to the German cities of Hannover and Hamm before reaching Aachen on the Germany-Belgium border. From Aachen first stop was Paris where I headed for Shinako and Ken's flat. My train had arrived in Paris early in the morning so

THE DECADE OF EUROPE – THE 1970S

unfortunately I found myself waking Shinako up at 09:00. Apparently she had been expecting me to arrive in the evening!

I was in Paris for a few days during which time I met up with my sister-in-law Peng and also Ken's parents. Apparently Ken's father was the Japanese Ambassador to Qatar. When I finally got back to London I had completed a journey of 2,356 km.

1979, the last year of the decade, was a quiet year for travel, perhaps because Fopin and I had decided that we should buy ourselves a flat in anticipation of getting married the next year. The lovely flat that we bought was one of seven flats in a small block in the lovely suburb of Wimbledon (which of course is world-famous for a certain tennis tournament).

The only record that I have for travel in 1979 was in March when Fopin and I had a short holiday in Paris where we met up with her sister Peng.

However, there was one other important happening in 1979. This was the visit of Fopin's mother and father to London. Fo's charming youngest sister Sichin also accompanied them. Somehow accommodation was found for all three of them in the house in Barons Court where Fo lived.

Fo's mother was a second generation Mauritian having

THE FINAL YEARS OF THE 1970S

been born there. Fo's father on the other hand was born in China and had left there by boat sailing out into the unknown. When the boat arrived in Mauritius he discovered that he liked the place so much that he decided it was to become his home.

Fo's father and I got along very well despite the fact that he was slightly deaf and neither of us could speak each other's language. Sometimes we went out on the underground or trains together and I pointed out things to be seen en route. On one occasion I took a group of five of us to the British Library where we joined a small tour. At one point on the tour we entered the famous Reading Room where many people were doing critical research for their personal projects. The guide, who was talking in a hushed voice, explained that under the ground and out of sight there were millions upon millions of books available for access. This info was conveyed to Fo's father who was so amazed at the numbers mentioned that he exclaimed his astonishment quite loudly in Creole, the language of Mauritius. We had to signal to him that he must please speak in a hushed tone!

And so life was about to change with the onset of the next decade!

Part III

Travels and Travails en Famille

28

The 1980s

How beautiful beyond compare, will paradise be found.
James Montgomery

The big event of 1980 was my marriage to one Fopin Li Kwong In, which happened on the 30th August. The service was held in the morning at the splendid National Trust property in Morden Park. This was followed by a midday wedding dinner at the Dog & Fox in Wimbledon Village. My best man was Graham, my travelling companion to Amsterdam and Yugoslavia back in 1974. In the evening the celebrations were completed by a gathering at the flat.

The wedding was something of an international gathering. Fo's mother came again from Mauritius once more with Sichin. From Germany were Minchoo and Eugen, their daughters Nadine and Nathalie and also Eugen's mother known as Mutti. All my friends in Australia had been invited but only one Aussie made it to the wedding and that was a certain Bruce Flood who was travelling in Europe at the time.

There were some important omissions. My sister Sylvia, her husband Atam, and their sons Justin, Adrian and Paul were unable to make it as they had been committed to a trip to the USA long before the announcement of the betrothal. My longest-time friend Tony Gomersal and his wife Diane could similarly not make it because they were also committed to an overseas holiday.

Apart from the omissions there also a family drama. It was planned that my brother Raymond would be bringing not only his wife Jean and our mum and dad, but also our youngest sister Christine. Then at the last minute he was suddenly struck down with an illness and Ray's son Steve had to step into the breach and bring them from Cornwall to London.

Once the wedding was over we spent a few days with our guests before Fo and I took off for our honeymoon to wonderful Amsterdam. Whilst there we stopped in the Hotel Vondel and in our wanderings I introduced Fo to the Heineken Brewery, Zeedijk (the Redlight District) as well as the Anne Frank House. We had a great experience one

THE 1980S

evening when we tried a dinner called rijsttafel which was a meal that contained 15+ dishes!!

What always impresses me in Amsterdam was that nearly everybody there speaks excellent English. Wouldn't it be great if we English could be just as proficient in other languages!

Although the eighties seemed to have been a relatively quiet decade for international travel it was nevertheless a very important decade in my life. After my marriage the next great event of the decade was the birth on October 4th 1981 of my daughter Zoe. Her birth was certainly one of the most exciting days of my life. I would run down to the hospital daily to see them. Although it doesn't happen any more, mother and daughter were kept in St Helier's Hospital for about one week, now they would be out in a day!

On 12th August 1983 Fo and I took Zoe on her first visit to France. We travelled by train from Victoria to Dover, followed by a ferry across to Calais and then finally another train to Paris. Although we stayed at the Hotel Rubun we did visit Shinako and Ken where Zoe tried to be over-friendly with their beautiful white cat which finally lost patience and snapped at Zoe. We returned to London on the 15th August but this time via Calais and Folkestone.

TRAVELS AND TRAVAILS EN FAMILLE

1985 was an important year because it was to be the year of my first visit to the island of Mauritius in the Indian Ocean. This was where Fopin had been born and where many of her family still lived.

We were flying with Air Mauritius and our neighbour Ted Clark drove us to Heathrow Airport. However when we got there Ted came back from a short walk to tell us that there was a problem with our plane. Apparently the plane was not in London waiting to fly us away but was in Paris with technical problems. As a consequence it would not be arriving in London until the next day. At this period Air Mauritius was a very minor airline and didn't have many planes. We managed to check our luggage in but then had to return to Wimbledon where gratefully we were hosted in the evening by Ted and his partner Tham.

The next day Fo, Zoe and I made our way again to Heathrow, this time by underground, to catch the plane anew. The plane journey was an exciting one as en route we were flying across the continent of Africa. Finally we arrived in Mauritius at the island airport which is in the south-eastern part of the island. We were met there by Sichin and her boss who was an extremely nice Japanese gentleman called Mr Okamoto. How it had been arranged I do not know, but Sichin advised us that her boss had

THE 1980S

Red Rocks, Mauritius

placed himself and his car at our assistance for the whole day. As a consequence of this, after dropping our luggage off at our Mauritian home he took us to a beautiful beach called Mon Choisy where Zoe and I took to the water. There Zoe began to scream with delight as very small fish came over to us and commenced swimming backwards and forward through her legs.

Fo's parents had a beautiful house in a village called Quatre Bornes where they lived with Sichin and the youngest sibling Taichong. The family had a dog but he did not live in the house as a pet, instead his function was as a guard dog. Loss of electricity could be a problem because sometimes it would cut out for hours. Also the rain, which seemed to come regularly in the early morning would pour down regularly in heavy bursts.

The island was beautiful and the people friendly, but I also sensed that there was a growing problem because more and more people were getting cars despite the fact that Mauritius was only a small island with a coastline of approximately 200 miles. Despite that reservation I still looked forward to the next visit.

1986 was to be another very exciting year because this was the year my son Maxim was born. Max was in a hurry to be born and has been in a hurry ever since. When his mother was taken to hospital on the morning of the 6th of August I had to drop Zoe off with friends Grace and Malcolm in nearby Morden and then rush to the hospital. I only just got to the hospital when Max arrived!!

Just one year later Maxim joined Fo, myself and Zoe on a short holiday in Ireland. On our first night there we wanted to go out briefly with the two children. Just across the way from our hotel we saw a smart pub. If this had been London we didn't think the staff would allow young children in at night but for some reason we thought we would try. I remember knocking on the door which was opened by the lady of the house. "We were wondering if we

THE 1980S

could come in with the young children" I asked hesitatingly. The lady smiled and said "Of course, please come in". It was a lovely evening in which I also learned of the care that the Irish take in serving their Guinness.

We had one moment of concern during the evening when Fo and I suddenly noticed that Max had disappeared. We looked around to see where he had gone. Finally we saw him. He had wondered off in the direction of the bar where some gents were sitting there enjoying their drinks, and one of them, seeing Max, had picked him up and held him in front of the bar and was explaining the workings of the bar to him. If only all pubs were as relaxed as this one!

My last big journey in the 1980s was in 1988 when we were to fly to the USA. At the beginning of the decade two of Fo's sisters were already living there.

Sister Nachin had been the first to leave Mauritius. She had been working as a nurse in Malagasy in 1969 when she met an American guy called Randy who was working in a US base there monitoring the first moon landing. When Randy returned to the USA Nachin went with him and they were to have three daughters: Debbie, Tina and Alysia. Randy and Nachin made a home in Brevard, North Carolina.

Nachin's older sister Yangchin was in Paris when she

TRAVELS AND TRAVAILS EN FAMILLE

also met an American citizen called Tashen who had been born in China. They married and lived for a period in California where Tashen worked for a university. After a period they made a decision to leave California to also make a home in Brevard where they opened a restaurant selling Chinese food. Like Nachin and Randy they also had three children, but in their case they were boys, Ming, Kwong and Ting.

In the early 1980s Fo's younger brother Taichong had left Mauritius to attend a US university. Following the death of Fo's father, Fo's mother, known as Popo, and Sichin went to North Carolina to make an home with Taichong. After their arrival this meant that four of Fo's siblings had made their home in the USA.

We did not meet Popo immediately after our arrival in Brevard as our presence was to be a big surprise at a birthday party that had been planned for her in a day or two. The party was being held in Yang and Tashen's restaurant so on the party day whilst Popo was made comfortable on a special chair in the restaurant we others were hidden away in the kitchen. At a certain point we were ushered in from behind her. The surprise was perfect!

Whilst in Brevard I was able to observe many aspects of American life. In the UK I had never seen guns being held in the open so it came as something of a shock to see a lady policewoman in the restaurant bearing a formidable looking weapon. Randy also said that he had a number of guns in his house. Whilst I was in Randy's house I was a bit hesitant to walk outside where I could clearly hear guns being fired nearby!

Another shock was to speak with a lady customer at the restaurant who told me that she had recently had to have an operation in a hospital but she had nearly needed to sell her house to pay for it! I suddenly felt grateful for having the NHS in the UK!

The holiday over we flew back across the Atlantic Ocean to London. **This was the first time I criss-crossed the Atlantic Ocean.** There were to be many transatlantic flights.

29

The 1990s – The First Half of the Decade

> *My daughter is not for sale!*
> Mike Harry

Sometime during the late 1980s and the early 1990s we four went to Zakynthos and Tunisia.

The main memory from Zakynthos is greeting the turtles as they emerged from the sea onto the nearby beach.

Three memories of Tunisia remain. The first is being invited for dinner at the home of a waiter that worked at a restaurant we patronised a few times. The second is the visit to Hannibal's home of Carthage. The third memory is being offered four camels for my daughter Zoe by another local gentleman. Of course I refused!

In 1991 we went to a city that has become one of my favourite places for a holiday, that is San Sebastian in

THE 1990S – THE FIRST HALF OF THE DECADE

Hannibal's Carthage

the north-west of Spain. The reason we first went there is because during the late 1980s we needed an au pair to look after Maxim whilst Fo and I worked and luck would have it that we found Yosune. Later when Yosune had returned to San Sebastian her younger sister Ainhoa also had a turn looking after the young Maxim.

We went to see where the sisters came from and stopped in the family home where their parents Sebastian and Maria lived with their brother Injake. Other visits followed, one to the wedding of Ainhoa to Colm, another to a second wedding of our Aussie friend Nicholas to San Seb girl Zuria. At least two other holidays have also been spent in this lovely city with its great atmosphere, beautiful beaches, and fantastic food including tapas, called pintxos there.

In 1992 we took a holiday to a country which I also came to love and would visit in the future whenever I could. That country is Thailand. Our neighbours Ted and Tham who lived two doors away from us in our street decided in 1991 to go and live in Tham's birth country of Thailand. We went there in 1992 to connect up with them again.

Tham, who was an architect by profession, owned two condominiums in Thailand, one in Bangkok and a second in the beautiful city to the north of Thailand called Chiang Mai. Whilst we were in Bangkok we stopped in the condominium there.

I loved the weather, the food and the people of Thailand, but the streets of Bangkok at that time were a shocker. The roads were not good and the traffic was horrendous. If you were in a car you were frequently caught up in an immense traffic jam which took ages to release. You just had to sit there and wait and wait. Rumours had it that parents driving their children to school also took breakfast and a toilet in the car for the use of their youngsters. One nice feature though were the small open sided vehicles called tuk tuks.

We enjoyed visiting the temples, palaces and restaurants of Bangkok before we went off with Ted and Tham to travel

THE 1990S – THE FIRST HALF OF THE DECADE

Elephant ride in Thailand

overnight by train to visit the 'condo' in Chiang Mai. For some unknown reason Fopin arrived at the condominium feeling very sick and we had to wait for a while on the ground floor until we felt able to take her up by lift to the condo. Fortunately she recovered well and we were able to go on and enjoy ourselves in this lovely city.

After a short time back in Bangkok we were taken south, this time by car, to Petburi where the King of Thailand was said to have his summer palace. Here we stopped in a bungalow owned by friends of Ted and Tham. One memory that stands out from that trip was our visit to the local market where I noticed a stall selling something called Jungle Curry. I am a lover of hot curries so I decided to give it a try, but my word was it hot!! I could only eat half of what I was given and eventually decided to stop eating it.

All good things come to an end so we said our goodbyes to Thailand knowing that we would return.

The big holiday of this decade was a trip down under to the land of Oz in 1995. We made one stop en route, at Singapore, where we boarded a second plane to Perth in Western Australia. When our plane touched down at Perth on July 26th I was back in the country that I had left some 24 years previously.

Perth has a reputation as being one of the sunniest cities in the world but strangely on the day that we arrived it was raining. We spent two nights at the Sullivans Hotel before leaving there on July 28th to start the unique experience of our holiday, crossing the Australian continent on a train called the Indian Pacific.

We had two twin cabins Max and I in one, Zoe and Fo in the other. It was easy to make friends on the train amongst the other passengers, most of whom were Aussie but there was a sprinkling of English and New Zealanders as well.

We made a short stop at Kalgoorlie at 23:00 before

THE 1990S — THE FIRST HALF OF THE DECADE

Crook in Cook

entering the Nullarbor Desert which stretched out 1000 km in front of us. Nullarbor gets its name from the Latin for tree [arbor] and less [null] which it is! And it was, of course, a train journey I had undertaken all those years before.

Eventually we arrived at a small township called Cook which is the origin of the saying in Australia "If you're crook, come to Cook". We got off the train and bought some souvenirs.

Passing Cook we came to the stretch of railway famous for being the longest stretch of straight railway in the world—some 478 km!! (Train drivers declare it a nightmare!). There was no sign of animal life.

Next stop was Tarcoola where Fo was delighted to be able to buy some dim sum (served with chips!). At 01:30 in the early hours of the morning we reached Port Augusta, eventually arriving at 06:00 in Adelaide, the capital city of the State of South Australia.

We were now within 24 hours of Sydney and the scenery was beginning to change from desert to green fields and trees.

The first stop in New South Wales was at Broken Hill where we had 15 minutes to stretch our legs before the Indian Pacific left mid-afternoon for the last 18 hours of travel to Sydney.

We arrived at Sydney, my old home, at 09:35, just 20 minutes late after a 68-hour journey. Some friends were there to welcome us. Along with Leo, Ian Bowie, Paul Clarke and Laurie Coleman there were Joan and Len, Laurie's parents.

We set off with Leo and Laurie to drive to Leo's home in Marsfield. As we crossed the Sydney Harbour Bridge I was able to detect many changes in the Circular Quay skyline and the North Shore. Later, after spending the day in Leo's home and locality, I joined Leo as he drove Laurie

THE 1990S – THE FIRST HALF OF THE DECADE

In Laurie's flat in Sydney

back to his home unit at McMahons Point. Laurie's flat was not only very comfortable but it had the most spectacular views looking out over Lavender Bay at Luna Park, the Harbour and the magnificent Harbour Bridge.

On the way back from Laurie's we made one last visit to end a long and momentous day when we went to look at my old pad at 31 Canberra Avenue, St Leonards. Memories of happy days—and nights—flooded back.

A couple of days later we went to see Sydney City and for lunch decided to head for Chinatown. It was then that one of those amazing coincidences occurred. The day previous we had called by the homes of Leo's nephews but they had not been there. Whilst we were in the restaurant Fo noticed someone that she recognised, it was none other than Nicholas who had chosen to have lunch not only in the same restaurant as us but on the same day and same time as us. With him were his cousin Michael and Michaels's son Yannis.

The next day Nicholas and Yannis came to take us on a trip to see some of the northern beaches. First stop was Palm Beach which delighted Zoe as she told us it was where "Home And Away" was filmed. Later we went on to see Manly Beach where I bought Maxim a boomerang, and myself a didgeridoo.

At 09:00 the next day Ian Bowie came to collect us to take us to Empire Bay where I would meet another old friend, Geoff Melville. En route we stopped at "Old Sydney Town" which was built as a replica of the 1788 settlement near the harbour. Later when we got to Empire Bay we met up with Geoff at his Real Estate shop and were then walked to his home where we met his lovely wife Jackie and their three children: Andrew, Luke and Felicity. Jackie had gone to a lot of trouble to feed a bunch of strangers. We were also joined by Geoff's mother, Bess, and Jackie's father Gerry. A lovely day.

THE 1990S — THE FIRST HALF OF THE DECADE

The next day we went to make the acquaintance of Leo's sister Marina. There we also met her husband Michael who had been born in the Greek island of Kalymnos. Nicholas and his younger brother Antony were of course there and later on when we made our way home we also met the eldest brother David. Over the next day we met up with Rosa and family and dined with Laurie's parents (my Aussie mum and dad!).

A couple of days later Leo drove us to Canberra the capital city of Australia where we stopped at the home of Peter and Sally Parsons. Peter and Sally were not there at the time, being of all places in Cambodia where Peter was working. Instead their third son Timothy was there with his charming wife Helen and they proved great hosts.

Before meeting a former colleague Brian Davoren for lunch we made a tour of the diplomatic embassies in Yarralumla. Outside the French Embassy there was a protest against the planned testing of nuclear bombs in the South Pacific. We met Brian at 12:30 and he took us for lunch in a restaurant that had formerly been a railway carriage. After lunch we went for a tour of the Houses of Parliament.

A few days later Paul (Clarke) treated us to a drive to the Blue Mountains, a hundred miles or so inland from the coast. At a place called Echo Point Paul tried to demonstrate the echo effect only to cause a Japanese tourist to appear to attempt hari-kari! To avoid an international incident, Paul and I moved away to the viewing point on the first of what are called the Three Sisters. The view was spectacular. After we had enjoyed some lunch we went on the scenic railway which goes deep into the valley. This railway was originally associated with coalmining in the valley and was claimed to be the steepest railway in the world! A very pleasant day. Thanks Paul.

The following day Nicholas treated the four of us to a trip to see *The Mikado* at the State Theatre. The show was excellent and included an outstanding Japanese Emperor. However, as we left the theatre we had a bit of a shock as Max told us that he had left his purse containing $60, on the floor beneath his seat. Max and I rushed back and were very lucky to meet an usher emerging from the theatre with Maxim's purse in his hand. Much relief.

On the Saturday afterwards a "30 Year Reunion of The Jubilee Park Tennis Club" was held at Paul and Carolyn Clarkes home. Most of the people that have already been mentioned were there but there were in addition John and Lyn Prince, Fred and Narelle Crump, Arthur Polkinghorne, Paul and Karmel Holloway and Mal Thatcher. Despite

THE 1990S – THE FIRST HALF OF THE DECADE

The Three Sisters, Katoomba

some of us putting on weight and some of us losing hair or greying it was very quickly just like old times and the interim 30 years had vanished. Paul's property was massive with giant trees and even a tributary of the Hawkesbury River flowing through it.

The hospitality continued the next day when we went with Leo and Laurie for a BBQ at the home of Ron and Dorothea Aquilina. Dorothea is a sister of Laurie. All of the five Aquilina offspring were there, all of whom, with the exception of John, had been born since I left Oz. Ron proved an excellent chef.

TRAVELS AND TRAVAILS EN FAMILLE

Another big get-together had been arranged at the North Sydney Leagues Club where I went with Leo and Laurie. Many old friends were there to meet me including Bill and Elizabeth Murphy, Barry Young, Fay Toome, Jenny Hill, Nola Nettheim, Geoff Dowe, Richard Murray, Gill Rogers and Col Ritchie. A great night was had by all.

Pleasure continued the next day. Mike Stephenson collected us and took us via his home, where we picked up Paula, to Bobbin Head in Kuringhai Chase. At midday we boarded a boat and motored up the Hawkesbury for 90 minutes before stopping at a quiet cove where we enjoyed a lunch of sandwiches that Mike and Paula had prepared. After lunch we motored some more before returning to our starting point where we returned the boat. The evening was spent at the Stephenson home where we met the Stephenson progeny Melinda, Jodie and Jeremy.

Our stay in Oz was sadly approaching an end. During this time my former colleague cum publisher Rosa took us to Botany Bay where Captain Cook had first landed. That was where it had all started! The next day Laurie brought us back to modernity when he took us to Luna Park where we indulged in the Big Dipper, the Tango and the Ferris Wheel.

Our last day in Australia was August 29th. We had one

special encounter just before we left for the airport when Ian Bowie brought his father to say hello (and of course goodbye). Ian's dad was a mighty looking 97 and still playing golf! He was to live on to the ripe old age of 104 during which time he was filmed for a documentary that interviewed men like him that had survived the terrible battles of World War 1.

When we got to the airport we found that we had accumulated so many souvenirs during our stay in Oz that it was necessary for us to store eight items in the hold. Nothing like this has ever happened since!

There were a lot of wonderful friends at the airport to see us off. After enjoying cappuccinos with them our farewells took so long that in the end we had to make a dash for the plane. Our wonderful Aussie holiday had ended.

30

The 1990s – The Second Half of the Decade

A worthy man is not mindful of past injuries.
Euripides

On July 30th 1996 we flew on an American Airlines flight from Gatwick Airport across the Atlantic Ocean, our destination being Charlotte, North Carolina. It was a long journey, flying first to Dallas before catching a second plane to Charlotte. We were travelling with Fo's sister Peng and her son Antony. Peng's hubby Jamie had been unable to come because of work demands. Disappointedly when we did get to Charlotte there was no sign of anyone waiting for us. It transpired that Sichin had somehow got confused and was expecting us at 23:00 instead of 21:00. She took a while to live this down.

When Sichin did arrive she was accompanied by her

mother Popo. Popo had been led to believe that they were at the airport to pick up Mauritian friends, so imagine her surprise and delight to see instead two more of her daughters as well as three grandchildren. Fortunately Taichong had also come along in a second car.

We drove to Tony and Sichin's home in Asheville where we took showers before eating an excellent meal cooked in advance by Popo and finally going to bed for a well-earned sleep.

The next day we met up with more of the family: another sister Agna and two of her daughters Alyssia and Tina. We also familiarised ourselves with the neighbourhood.

A few days later we visitors were informed to prepare for a long journey by road to Orlando in Florida. Tony and Sichin had hired a large, air-conditioned truck for this journey. At 09:30 on Friday August 2nd nine of us set off on a car journey that I had been informed was 586 miles long. This was perhaps a distance not uncommon in the USA but nevertheless strange to us English! We arrived at Orlando approximately 11 hours later.

On our first day in Orlando we went to Universal Studios where we tried many of the amazing rides. The favourite for me, and for Tony, Zoe, Antony and Maxim, was called Back To The Future. We liked it so much that we went back for a second go which proved even more frightening than the first!

On day two we went to the Magic Kingdom which we enjoyed despite the temperature rising to 95°F. One of the rides, called Space Mountain, was the most frightening rollercoaster ride I have ever been on. While we were waiting to board we could observe the ride cars high above us appearing as meteors flashing through the night sky. During the ride itself however, some of the drops were almost vertical and ended with gut-wrenching right-angle turns at the bottom. My stomach was severely tested.

Although some of the younger members of our party showed signs of stress, Popo, who was 77-years-old, stood up to both the heat and the walking magnificently. The next day we made the journey back to Asheville in a slightly quicker time than the journey south had been.

The next day, August 6th, was to prove a momentous day! My first injury in the USA and my first experience of a USA hospital! It was also Maxim's birthday.

At midday Agna's daughter Debbie arrived with her then boyfriend Paul after which a decision was made to go to a place called Sliding Rock near Brevard. I had seen Sliding Rock on previous visits to the USA but had not felt tempted to try the sliding experience out on those occasions. On this occasion however all of us were planning to take the slides except for Agna and Peng.

To take the ride, you first walked through the fast flowing water to where the stream becomes a torrent, at which point you seat yourself as comfortably as you can on your butt. After that you are soon whizzing over the rocks, sometimes bumping up and down, until finally you take off into space to splash down into the cool water in the pool at the foot of the slide.

I tried this slide twice at which point I decided I had done enough sliding. However I was told by Peng that I must try again as she wanted to take a photo of all of us sliding down one after another, from the youngest to the oldest (me!). I now wish I hadn't been persuaded.

Everything went well till it was my turn. I sat down, started sliding in the right direction, ie the right, but unfortunately bounced off a camber which propelled me in a leftward direction. I finally splashed down in the pool with my hands down by my sides, fingers pointing down. Suddenly I had a nasty shock as my fingers struck a rock. When the rock wouldn't move, my fingers did! Coming to the surface I knew that I had a problem because the normally straight fingers of my left hand now showed the two middle fingers pointing in opposite directions – sideways from the middle of the fingers!

I noticed that there were life guards around the pool so I held up my damaged hand to catch their attraction. It caught their attention alright, but they thought I was waving to them so they waved right back! Fortunately there were other people around the pool who had been more observant so a couple of them called out "there is a man injured". The life guards then realised their error and came in and helped me out of the water.

Peng and Zoe accompanied Agna and I to the local hospital. I arrived there in swimming trunks and a damp t-shirt so after recording my personal details at the reception desk the pleasant staff showed me where I could get changed whilst a doctor was found.

Following X-Rays the doctor was able to inform me that my fingers were not broken but dislocated. Eventually he got hold of my hand and pulled the fingers straight again. Fortunately Zoe was allowed to keep me company whilst all this was happening. Finally a splint was put on my hand and I was told that I could leave. Apparently the staff had commended me for being so calm and said I was "a real trooper".

Just before I left the hospital I stopped at the reception

desk and asked the nice ladies there "this being the USA, I think I have to pay some money, don't I?". Yes, I was told. I thought that they were going to tell me the equivalent of say £100, but I was very shocked when they told me the equivalent of £630!! I paid with my credit card and later recovered 90% of it through travel insurance. However, my final thought was (again not for the first time) "thank goodness for the NHS!" I was driven back to South Oaks Circle where I was welcomed as the wounded hero.

The next day I began the process of getting used to having only one usable hand. At the start of the day I found difficulty shaving and showering and later in the day I was prevented from swimming. That apart, thinking back I could only be thankful that the injury wasn't worse. I could of course have damaged my right hand preventing writing … and worse. It could have been an injury to the spine. I hate to think what the cost of hospitalisation would have been for that. Once again, thank goodness for the NHS.

On August the 6th Maxim was able to celebrate his 10th birthday in the USA and the Republican Convention came up on the 12th August when Bob Dole announced that his running mate against Bill Clinton would be Jack Kemp.

A few days later Tony took us to his favourite State,

Tennessee, also the home of his university, the University of Tennessee.

When it rains in North Carolina it really rains! On one occasion Zoe had an appointment at the hairdresser and I was required to stay with her. Whilst waiting there was a tremendous storm with an horrendous downpour of rain. It was so torrential that visibility was reduced to only a few yards and the car park outside the hairdresser's began to look like a lake.

We left the USA on Monday August 26th arriving London Gatwick on the 27th where a pre-arranged taxi awaited us and we managed (just) to get all our suitcases in the car, either in its boot or else tied to the roof!

* * *

In August of 1997 the family went on a holiday to the island of Tenerife, the largest island in the group known as the Canary Islands. The island is 794 square miles in area approximately 26 miles east to west across the centre and 27½ miles north to south. In the 15th century the island was conquered by the Spanish and the island's currency when we went there were Spanish pesetas. It is said that in 1936 General Franco met fellow army officers in Tenerife to plan the coup attempt which was to lead to Spain's bitter civil war.

Our plane was to leave from Gatwick at the ridiculously early hour of 06:40 so we all had to be up by 03:00 to be ready for the taxi. Disappointingly the arrival at Tenerife was chaotic and we had to wait ages for our luggage. Eventually however they arrived and we were able to board a coach that took us to our hotel, the Mare Verde Apts in Playa de Las Americas.

At the hotel Max got very enamoured of the slides that connected the four swimming pools together. An unfortunate reaction to his enthusiasm however was that he became sunburnt on his shoulders.

The highest point in the island is Mount Teide which at 12,199 feet tall is also the highest point in all of Spain and its possessions. The population of the island was 600,000 at this time, of which 220,000 were in the capital city of Santa Cruz. The north of the island contains much more vegetation than the south where it is altogether hotter and drier.

We English had some difficulty adjusting to the shopping hours which were from 10:00 to 13:30 when it closed for lunch (Siesta) to reopen again at 17:00 before closing at 20:30.

Misfortune struck one day when Maxim came back late

in the day from the hotel pools somewhat tearful because he had broken a large chip off his front tooth. We tried to find a dentist for him but there were none available at the time. Max was not in pain so we had to leave it till the next day when a local staff man referred us to a nearby dentist who examined Maxie's teeth and did an x-ray. The x-ray showed a dark patch which he said was the result from a blow. He prescribed antibiotics for Max which he had to take every six hours.

The most memorable and pleasant of the three excursions that we went on in Tenerife was a boat trip to see the whales and the dolphins. We were collected by a coach and taken to a local port where we boarded a catamaran with a four man crew. After a short sail we saw the dolphins which delighted everybody as they undulated in and out of the water near our boat. After a while we were informed that we would move into deeper waters to seek out the whales. However, it seemed to take so long that I began to doubt that we would ever see any whales. But suddenly there they were, about six to seven of them! It was a delight to see these magnificent creatures, a couple of which came right up beside our boat before disappearing under the waves.

Zoe appeared to have won another heart as the young guide took a shine to her, called her beautiful, and said he

THE 1990S – THE SECOND HALF OF THE DECADE

was falling in love with her. Fo on the other hand was not feeling so good as she became seasick. In the end however a crew member became aware of her mal-de-mer and provided an unusual cure—a bucket of cold water thrown over her head, and it worked!

Eventually it was time to leave this lovely island and we returned to London suntanned and full of memories.

* * *

On the 14th February 1998 we four had to be in the USA again for a very special occasion being the wedding of Sichin to Tony. Zoe was a bridesmaid and Maxim was the ring boy.

The marriage to Sichin and Tony

Later in the year, during the school holidays in August, we flew from Gatwick to Rimini in North-Eastern Italy from where we were coached to the Hotel Plaza in Cattolica.

Maxim felt really rich in Italy because he had a 100,000 lira note. Richness was an illusion however because the Euro had not yet been introduced to Italy and at that time one sterling pound exchanged for 2,813 lira! Maxim's 100,000 lira note was worth roughly £35.

A couple of days after our arrival we took a coach to San Marino which had a population then of only 21,000. San Marino is the smallest republic in the world and is surrounded by Italy. It was a great place for shopping.

After another few days in Cattolica we got up early to get a coach to the picturesque city of Venice. Unfortunately we had not been on the coach very long before we realised that Maxim was not feeling very well. Nevertheless he was very stoical and did not complain despite the fact that he began vomiting.

Eventually we got to Sottomarina where we left the coach and caught a launch called Palladio to Venice. The launch trip would have been very enjoyable if it were not for our continuing concern for Maxim who kept bringing up everything he ate and drank.

When we got to Venice we walked over six bridges that

brought us to Piazzo San Marco where we took a gondola. Our gondolier resembled the Australian actor, Brian Brown. Maxim continued to impress us. Although feeling awful, he soldiered on, even apologizing when he was sick. Later we were able to give Maxie a sickness pill which enabled him to sleep some of the launch trip back to where we re-caught the coach. Two days later on August the 6th Max celebrated his 12th birthday and we took him to a recommended fish restaurant where the birthday boy really enjoyed the food having got over his illness.

Shortly after that Maxim made a friend of a boy of his own age called Jani who had newly arrived at the hotel with his family from Rotterdam. The two boys were inseparable until the day of our departure on August 11th.

The final trip before the new millennium was another visit in 1999 to the paradise that is Mauritius.

Part 4

Travels into the New Millennium

31

New Orleans and the Lost Luggage Saga

Let me not know that all is lost.
Canto

We were off to another wedding! This time it was in the magical city of New Orleans where Debbie and Paul were getting married.

We were due to leave by Delta Airlines flight DL059 from Gatwick at 11:30 on Friday December 15th. Amazingly we were still expected to arrive in New Orleans in sufficient time that evening for the traditional get-together held the night before the wedding. Consequently we made sure we were at the airport by 09:00 to ensure collection of our boarding passes.

At 10:30 we were listening out for the advice informing us to go to the gate to board the plane. We waited and waited but it did not come. We enquired at Information only to be told that they did not know either.

Finally (11:15?) the call came to go to the gate only to be told by a very embarrassed Delta Airlines lady that our plane had been overbooked!! She went on tell us that the only way the plane would leave was if 30 or so passengers volunteered to miss this flight and agree to go on a later flight. Those that did volunteer would be put up at a hotel near the airport, meals included, and in addition would receive a substantial amount of spending money.

The spending money offered was of such a large amount that perhaps we would have considered accepting it if it wasn't for the fact that we were expected to be at the evening function in New Orleans. Consequently we did not volunteer to stop in London overnight. Fortunately others did and eventually we boarded our plane and it took off two hours late at 13:30.

Our plane landed 16:00 in Atlanta and we went to check in for the final plane that was going to take us to New Orleans. The gentleman at the desk gave us our boarding passes, smiled at us, and wished us a good journey. Unfortunately as we started to walk away he suddenly called us back. We were told that he had just got notice that our plane was being delayed. We were referred to a waiting room.

NEW ORLEANS AND THE LOST LUGGAGE SAGA

The evening disappeared with no call to board. People were getting really angry. Around 23:00ish we were told by another lot of embarrassed staff that the lights at New Orleans Airport had failed and as a consequence we wouldn't be flying there that night. Instead we were told to board coaches that would take us to hotels where we could sleep. This was a bad joke however as we were due back at the airport for 06:30ish in the morning. The coach journeys there and back took a good 30 minutes or more so I thought that it would be best if I kept awake whilst the others napped.

When we got back to Atlanta Airport that morning it at first appeared that we wouldn't be among those passengers on the first plane out of there to New Orleans. This was too much so I had to talk very forcibly to the staff that we must be on the first flight. I pointed out that we had been on a much delayed flight from the UK followed by a non-flight the previous evening. We had already missed out on the previous evening's function and further if we didn't get to New Orleans soon we might even be missing out on the wedding as well. They agreed we deserved priority and we were allowed to go on the first plane. We thought our troubles were over, but we were mistaken!!

We arrived at New Orleans and waited for our five

cases of luggage to appear but none of it did! There was one case for each of us and a fifth case that was full of gifts for family members. We waited and waited watching case after case passing through but none of ours appeared. Zoe was distraught, telling us that her case contained £1,000 of clothing, something we were a little dubious about.

Finally we had to give up waiting. We were assured that we would be informed when our cases arrived so we had no choice but to leave for our hotel. Zoe was in tears.

The hotel was very comfortable but Zoe refused to leave it until her luggage was found. In the meantime we met up with family members and Fopin and Maxim were able to get loans of clothes from the family to attend the wedding. Unless our luggage was found Zoe and I could only go to the wedding in the clothes we had travelled in. I was prepared to go so-dressed but Zoe refused to go to the wedding unless she could get at the clothes in her case.

Late afternoon and there was still no word. Fo and Maxim got dressed for the wedding but Zoe affirmed that there was no way she was going. Suddenly however we got notice that two of our cases were at the airport so Zoe and I went off in a taxi hoping that the cases would turn out to be hers and mine.

When we saw the cases, one was my suitcase and the

other was the case full of gifts. Fopin's and Maxim's cases were not there and of course neither was Zoe's. The Delta Airways Officer agreed to pay for the taxis and also gave us a pack of dollars somewhere in excess of £100 to buy some emergency clothing.

Zoe and I returned to the hotel, I got dressed but Zoe still refused to attend. Reluctantly I left her there and set off to find the wedding venue. I had briefly seen it in the morning but I could not remember how to get there so I tried at least four hotels before I found the one where the wedding reception was being held.

As I walked into the hotel towards the reception area I was surprised to see my two nephews from Oxford, Justin and Paul, walking towards me. "Uncle you have missed it, it's all over" I was told. That said, they were kind enough to go back into the hall and bring me out an alcoholic drink to satisfy my thirst.

The next morning we went out into the city to buy some clothes for Zoe with the money given us at the airport. Having done that, when we got back to our hotel in the afternoon we were delighted to find that the three remaining suitcases had been delivered there during our absence. Zoe now had another £100 of clothing on top of the £1,000 in the suitcase!

We enjoyed the remainder of our stay in this delightful city before returning to London for Christmas. I claimed compensation from Delta Airways for the debacle, of which more later.

32

Travelling Again! North-Eastern USA

For my part I travel not to go anywhere, but to go. I travel for travel's sake. The great affair is to move.
Robert Louis Stephenson

Things were about to change!

In the 1960s my travel was very much the way Robert Louis Stephenson has described, long journeys so that the scenery is different every day: the six week sea journey from Southampton to Sydney, and the monumental journey with my friend Leo across two continents, Asia and Europe, were features of that time!

In the 1970s, my "Decade Of Europe", I also made many journeys travelling on my own but meeting and stopping with friends sometimes en route.

Things changed in the next two decades, (which I have previously described) because then we travelled as a foursome and usually visited just one city where we enjoyed everything that that city could provide.

As we entered the new millennium things were beginning to change: Zoe and Maxim were getting older and beginning to plan their own holidays. There were still going to be some family holidays together however, mainly involving Fopin and me, but some that also involved Zoe and Max. That said the next seven years were going to be highlighted by three very long journeys, one of which I was to share with my son Max.

The first of these long journeys was initiated by the fact that I turned 60 in June of 2001. I had many times expressed my interest in travelling by train in the USA and my dear wife Fopin, remembering this, offered to buy me as a 60th birthday present a ticket for unlimited rail travel in North-Eastern USA. As a consequence I set off at 13:10 on the 17th July from London Gatwick heading for the city of Boston.

I arrived Boston at 15:40 on the same date (the USA being behind us in time!) and was met at the airport by Juli, the partner of my nephew Adrian. After first taking me back to their address in Thorndike Street in 'Cambridge' Juli then treated me to an evening meal at the Casa Portugal.

The next day Juli and I took the train to the centre of Boston and whilst Juli went off to work I went shopping for jeans and trainers which seemed so much more cheaper in Boston than in London. At 13:00 I met Juli again and after a lunch we walked on to Chinatown before going to a bar. Here I had my second surprise of the day – when Juli ordered some drinks from the barmaid she was asked apologetically to prove that she was old enough to purchase alcohol (she was I think 26 at the time!).

I was heading off on the train in the evening so I asked Juli if she could drop me early at the Boston South rail station. Lucky I did! It turned out that for some obscure reason all my train reservations had been cancelled. Fortunately a friendly and efficient staff member corrected these errors after which Juli and I had cappuccinos together before I boarded the train at 20:45.

The train was very spacious and comfortable and I was able to relax and enjoy the journey. Leaving Boston, we passed through Rhode Island, New Haven, Bridgeport, New York, New Jersey, Philadelphia and Washington before finally arriving at Richmond in Virginia at 08:54 in the morning.

I had to wait at Richmond to catch a train at 12:37 that was going to take me even further on into North Carolina.

During this part of the journey there was a great drama in my carriage. I was suddenly disturbed by some agonising cries coming from behind me in the carriage. I and all the passengers nearby stood up and looked back to see the cause of the cries. What we saw was a man choking and his wife screaming for help. At that point help came—a well-built black gentleman had got to his feet, gone to the choking gentleman, lifted him up, grasped the man from behind and managed to relieve whatever was causing the choking by pulling him sharply from behind aka the Heimlich Manoeuvre). Well done that hero who may have saved a man's life that day!

The train left the State of Virginia to enter North Carolina where it passed through Greensboro before arriving at my destination Charlotte.

I caught a taxi to the Park Hotel Suite which my lovely sister-in-law Yang had not only booked for me but also paid for me. At the time Yang was in this hotel attending a teaching course so as a consequence I was not to see her until she and two other lady teachers came knocking at my door at 23:00. After our greetings I was informed that I would see her next at 11:15 in the morning after the finale to the teaching course.

Apparently one of Yang's course mates Kim lived near

Morganton where we would be heading and Kim told us that she would be happy to drive us there. Many thanks Kim.

Arriving in Morganton we found Yang's mother Popo and Yang's youngest son Ting in the house. Tony, Sichin and their daughter Isabelle were out when we arrived but were to return shortly after. That evening Popo cooked a great meal for all of us.

The next day I went to Hickory with Sichin, Tony and Ting where I bought another set of jeans and also gifts for Fo, Zoe and Max. This was followed by a hot dog lunch. Back home I watched the great film *Dirty Dancing* which had been filmed in nearby North Carolina.

The day after, Sunday July 9th, I said farewell to Popo, Sichin and Tony, after which Ting drove Yang and me to Greensboro where we dropped Yang off to attend a Teachers Workshop.

Leaving Greensboro Ting and I motored to Chapel Hill where we first did a tour of the University of Carolina before collecting Ting's brother Kwong. Later that evening we three were joined by a family friend Beth for a Chinese restaurant meal before going to Ting's flat for a well-earned sleep.

The next day after breakfast at McDonalds Ting drove

me back to Greensboro where I was to catch the 09:44 train for the long journey to New York.

I became a little concerned as we approached New York because the train was running one hour late and the plan was to meet my nephew Adrian at Penn Station. After we met we had to catch a late train to a place called Convent where he lived. Luckily we got there without losing any more time and the very patient Adrian was there to meet me.

We moved quickly to the platform for the Convent train which luckily was still there. At Convent we had a short walk in dark surroundings to the campus building where Adrian had a flat.

Adrian accompanied me the next morning to Convent Station where he saw me safely on the train that was going to take me to Penn Station in New York.

Arriving at Penn Station I purchased a One Day Travelcard for the Subway and made my way to South Ferry where I caught a ferry that took me first to the magnificent Statue Of Liberty and then on to Ellis Island. At Ellis Island I tried to search for Harry relatives but to no avail. Most of the morning had disappeared after that so I returned to South Ferry.

Leaving South Ferry I was becoming very hungry so

TRAVELLING AGAIN! NORTH-EASTERN USA

I decided to walk till I found a café cum restaurant where I could sit down at a table, have waiter service, and enjoy, say, a pizza with a large glass of cold beer. It became frustrating, because sometimes there were cafes where you had to stand, and at other times restaurants where there was either no waiter service or didn't serve beer. My appetite was becoming intense so I decided to ask a young man who was standing outside his office smoking. "Sorry to bother you, but where can I found a restaurant where …". The fellow suddenly said "Yes, just around the corner in the Twin Towers". I don't remember being aware of the Twin Towers at that point possibly because I was walking at the foot of large offices anyway. Saying thank you I moved on and lo and behold coming round the corner there was a great looking restaurant on the ground floor of the first tower I reached.

Some of my previous desires were put on hold however as for instance I had to queue to place my order and I chose not to have a pizza after seeing a baguette full of what looked like delicious contents. However I was able to sit at a table near a window and was also able to enjoy the best beer that I had tasted in the USA during the holiday so far.

As I ate I was able to enjoy the view. Through the windows I could see people sitting at various places gossiping and enjoying the warm weather. Looking at the other tower I saw an orchestra on the ground floor playing great music for everyone's enjoyment. As I ate and drank I enjoyed the experience for probably an hour and a half.

Finally leaving, I made my way to Chinatown passing the attractive Woolwich Building en route. Then on to the Empire State Building where I paid $9 to travel to the viewing area on the 86th floor. The views were stupendous.

I returned to Penn Station to meet up with Adrian and from there we made our way to the Little Korea area where we found a good restaurant. After the meal we headed back home to Convent. By the time I got there I was very tired from the days heat, humidity and walking.

The next day I took the train again to Penn Station and after visiting Times Square I snacked at the station, before returning to Convent where we were joined at 17:30 by Juli arriving from Boston. In the evening we were invited to the home of Adrian's colleague Bruce where we were treated to a BBQ. After a very pleasant evening the rain arrived.

The next day was to be my last day in New York but this day I was to have the pleasure of Juli's company. We took the subway to 103rd Street (how many streets do they have in New York?) where we entered the great park known as Grand Central Park. Later after walking the full length of the park and eating a meal at a restaurant claiming to be "the best salad bar in New York" we returned to Convent where I packed and showered in readiness for my return to Boston.

That night I caught a train leaving at 01:30 for Boston where on arrival I made my way to Adrian and Juli's flat and let myself in with the key that they had given me. After a relaxing day I caught the 18:10 plane back to London, holiday over!

There was a very dramatic event that followed this holiday. A few weeks later I was at home doing some work supporting my occupation as a private mathematics tutor when my lovely wife Fopin rang me up from her office to tell me to go and look at the television as there had been a plane crash!

"I'm sorry dear" I said, "I am very busy and there are plane crashes every day". Fo remained adamant though and in the end I relented and went to the lounge and turned on the television, just in time to see a second plane crashing into the Twin Towers ... I remained there for hours as I witnessed the horror unfold. At some time the Towers collapsed and with it my memories of a restaurant and lovely lunch were grounded into oblivion.

33

The Trans-Canadian

Travel, and change of place, impart vigour.
Seneca

In 2003 my son Maxim expressed a willingness to travel with me on one of the longest train journeys in the World, that is on the Trans-Canadian from Vancouver to Montreal. A real father-son bonding exercise! Our plane left from London Gatwick Airport on the 7th August at the early hour of 10:25 and arrived Vancouver 40 minutes early at 13:50 (time difference to UK—eight hours).

My sister-in-law Yang Chin who had been so helpful on my North-Eastern USA trip was also very helpful on this holiday as she had arranged introductions to Mauritian friends of hers who said that they were happy to provide accommodation for Max and me in Vancouver. As a consequence, father Michel and daughter Wendy were waiting for us at Vancouver airport. After greetings we were driven

THE TRANS-CANADIAN

to the lovely suite flat where they lived in 3588 Vanness Avenue (why do properties in the USA and Canada have numbers going into thousands!). At the flat we met mother Rosemay, another daughter Jenny and son Michael. We were to meet the third daughter Karen later.

The next day we were taken out to see something of Vancouver by Rosemay and Jenny who proved great guides. They suggested that we purchase one day travelcards which would enable us to travel freely all day not only on the buses and trams but also on the sky train and sea bus. Amongst the activities we enjoyed that day were a great lunch at the wonderful Old Spaghetti Factory Restaurant and a sea bus journey to visit the Lonsdale Quay Market.

We had one big worry though! We had travelled thousands of miles to Vancouver where we planned to board a train which was to take us through the Rocky Mountains. This train would transport us out of the Province of British Columbia and then on into Alberta. The bad news however was that there was a very large fire in the Rocky Mountains area that could possibly lead to cancellation of the train!

Over the next two days we enjoyed the great city of Vancouver with the assistance of our wonderful hosts during which time we were happy to be reassured that the train would not be cancelled.

On the 10th August we were taken to the very busy railway station and found it full of people. Max and I were among the last to board the train but our fellow travellers and the staff were friendly so this boded well for a good trip. Although the train was scheduled to leave at 17:30 it did not leave till much later. Finally, however, we left Vancouver with thousands of miles of rail journey ahead of us to experience.

During the evening we left British Columbia and entered the Canadian Province of Alberta. By 1200 the next day we were travelling through the majestic beautiful mountains that bear the name Rocky Mountains. They were an amazing sight!

In early evening the train stopped at Edmonton the capital city of Alberta. As we were not stopping there overnight the train shortly continued on, moving into flatter country that was a great contrast to the mountainous scenery that we had been seeing up until Edmonton. During the night the train entered the Province of Saskatchewan passing through its largest city Saskatoon.

On the 12th August we left Saskatchewan and entered Manitoba, the fourth Province on our journey. Here Max and I left the train at Winnipeg, the capital of the Province, and caught a taxi to our hotel. We liked the Delta Winnipeg where our first priority were showers followed by exercise in the gym. During the afternoon we did some shopping finishing the day at the Asahi Japanese Restaurant.

The next day we had breakfast at the Pancake House in the Forks Centre because Canadian hotels don't do breakfast! After looking over this Centre we took a bus to another Centre, the Polo Park Centre, where Max bought himself some new trainers. The day finished with an excellent buffet dinner at an Indian restaurant.

We were leaving Winnipeg on the 14th August. For breakfast I went out and purchased bagels for Max and myself. As a result of this I established something of a passion for them to carry into the future.

At 10:45 we took a taxi to the station to catch the train which was due in at 11:20 to be ready for a 12:25 departure. That said the train arrived late and left late. Whilst we were waiting Max and I used a phone card to contact Toronto, Montreal and Fopin back in London.

Once the train got underway we discovered the food service on it was abysmal and the restaurant manager was something of a grump.

Late in the afternoon the train left Manitoba and entered the Province of Ontario and the scenery became a vista of endless lakes, first Lake Superior then Lake Huron.

The driver on this train had something of a wild sense of humour and announced that our destination Toronto was blacked out by a power failure which made Max and I wonder what was ahead of us.

The train arrived on time at the Grand Union Station, Toronto at 20:00 and we got a taxi to the Delta Chelsea Hotel. We had been informed that this hotel was the biggest hotel in Canada. When we got there we found that there were certainly power difficulties - although there were lights there was no air conditioning. This was disturbing because the day temperature in Toronto was a very hot 95°F. However one very strange thing that we learned was, whilst it was excessively hot for us in Toronto, it was even hotter for Fopin and Zoe in London! Apparently whilst we were in Toronto our home city London was experiencing it's hottest ever day with a temperature over 100°F!!!!

Although smaller than the room that we had in Winnipeg our room in Toronto was nice. Max and I showered then went for a meal and a walk around the block where we were happy to find a 24-hour food store nearby. Back in our room we had a phone call from Sandya. Once again a sister-in-law had improved the opportunities for our holiday. This time it was Sichin who had contacted good Mauritian friends of hers called

Sandya and Iqbal. Sandya rang to tell us that they would be coming at 11:00 the next morning to take us to Niagara Falls. What a treat.

The next morning Fo rang at 05:45 because she had heard about the blackout in Toronto and she was worried. I reassured her that we had survived. Sandya also phoned to tell us that the pickup would have to be delayed a little until 13:00 because Iqbal had to work in the morning. This gave me time to get myself a haircut.

Iqbal drove us to Niagara via the steel town of Hamilton where we took a lunch break. Also en route we stopped for a look at Fort George, a British fort that had been built to protect Canada from the American settlers!!

Niagara Falls was absolutely amazing. There are actually two Falls, one called the American Falls, the other a larger horseshoe-shaped Falls called the Canadian Falls. Iqbal told us that they had planned to show us a view of the Canadian Falls from a viewing chamber behind the falling water, however this had become impossible because the blackout had necessitated the diversion of water to the hydro-electric facility.

After a fascinating day traffic jams delayed our journey back to Toronto and as a consequence we arrived back at our hotel after midnight.

The next day was a more relaxed day. I woke at 07:00 but Max didn't wake until 12:00. Once Max had showered and got himself dressed we found a McDonalds for a light lunch.

At 15:30 we met Iqbal who took us to a shopping mall to pass the time before we went to collect Sandya from her work. When we were all together we went for a buffet meal at an Indian restaurant then drove to nearby Oakville to see the gardens there. After a visit to the beach of Lake Ontario we were taken back to our hotel where we started packing in preparation for our departure from Toronto the following day. As they left us we thanked Iqbal and Sandya for being such splendid hosts.

The next morning we left by taxi at 10:00 to get the train on to our last destination Montreal. This was the shortest of the rail journeys in Canada for us, leaving Toronto at 11:30, soon after crossing the border into the Province of Quebec, and finally arriving in its largest city Montreal a little late at 16:46. We were met at the station by Adrian who took us on the Metro to his local station of Mont-Royal.

When we got to Adrian's flat we had only been there five minutes when Fopin rang. Shortly after that Juli arrived home from work. That evening we four went to an excellent Portuguese restaurant where I feasted on a great "Portuguese Steak".

On the morning of the 19th July went off to Uni to study whilst Adrian went to his tutor job at the famous McGill University. Somewhat later Max and I went out to see Montreal, first by walking to McGill University. As we walked I was a little concerned about being in Quebec at the time because there was then a strong movement to make Quebec a French offshoot rather than for it remaining as a former English colony. Consequently I wondered if the Quebec citizens would be a little unfriendly towards those who were obviously English. However I was completely mistaken because as far as I can recollect everybody we spoke to was friendly and helpful.

After a lunch with Adrian and Juli, Max and I went off to get him some art supplies and to make our first journey alone on the Metro. Montreal seems to have a broad range of restaurants and our first day there finished with a great meal at a Tibetan restaurant.

The next day Max and I relaxed around the flat before taking lunch at the Santrapol Sandwich Café. After lunch Max returned to the flat to do some Art Project Work whilst I set off to climb Mont-Royal.

Unfortunately somewhere en route up Mont-Royal I

took a wrong path which caused to me to arrive at the top of the mountain with a sweat-drenched shirt. After resting and enjoying the view for a while I wondered if there was an easier route down the mountain. However the Montreal folks came good as I was lucky enough to meet some very helpful people. One Chinese gentleman showed me the right path down, and a little later a policewoman even offered me a ride on her horse! Finally there was a young woman who told me that she had enjoyed a great holiday in Birmingham, England and was happy to show me to the bus stop where I caught a bus.

You would have thought that I had already had enough exercise for one day but in the evening Adrian persuaded Max and I to go on a bicycle ride through Chinatown and along the canal. When I got back to the flat another shirt was drenched!

By contrast, the two remaining days were relatively relaxing, some dietary highlights being a meal in an Ethiopian restaurant with Adrian and a substantial dim sum lunch in Chinatown that Max and I shared. I don't know if it is still the case but prices in Canada at that time did not include sales tax in the displayed price, instead you find the price increased when paying!

On August 23rd Max and I flew out from Montreal

THE TRANS-CANADIAN

Airport at 20:45 arriving London Gatwick at 07:45 the next day. The end of a great holiday! And it also meant that **I had completed rail journeys by rail in the Northern hemisphere all around the world.**

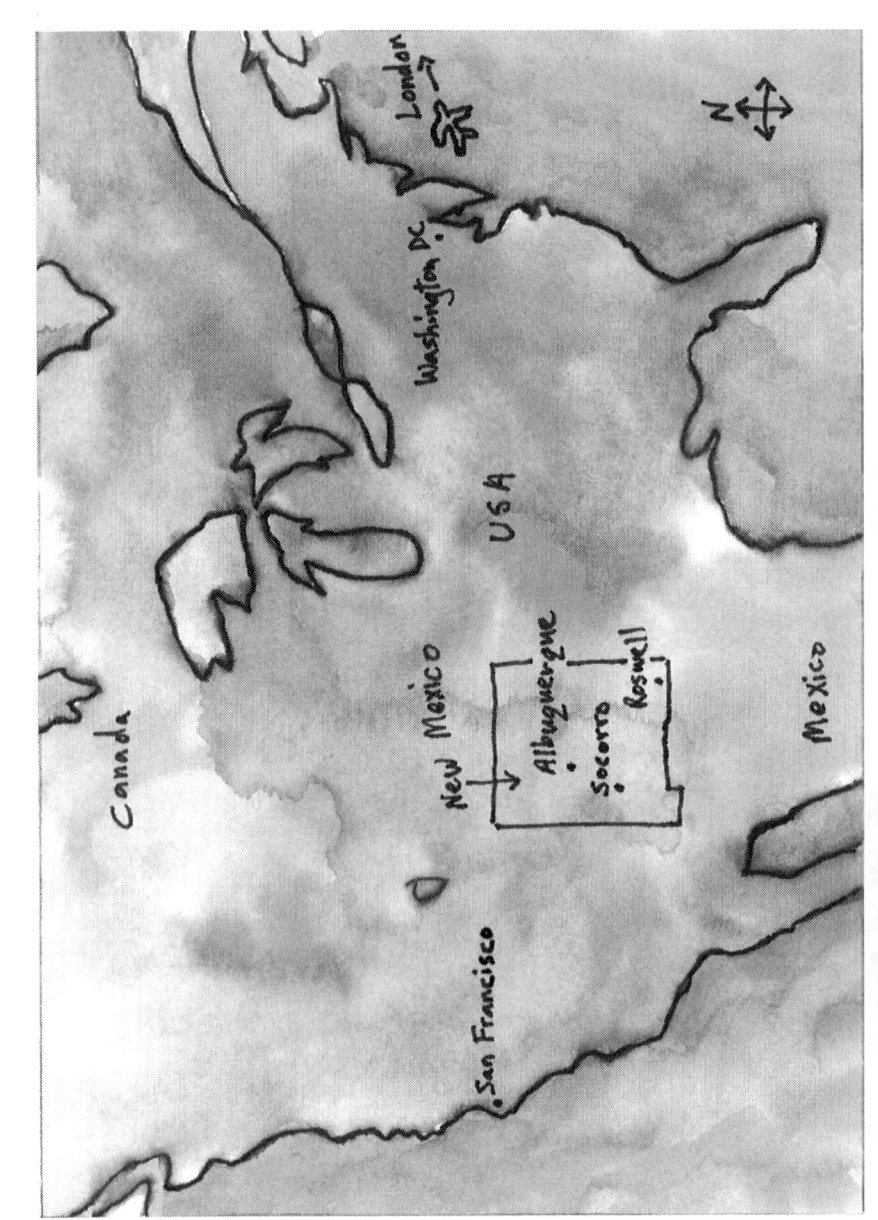

34

The End of the Journey

Here is my journey's end.
Shakespeare

At some point in the years after the Trans-Canadian trip I came to a realisation that I had not only travelled around the world by sea, achieved in journeys to and from Australia in 1961 and 1971, but I had also travelled around the world by land, first through Asia and Europe in 1970, then later by the journeys through North-Eastern USA and Canada in 2001 and 2003. In contrast however, although it may be true that travelling around the World by air may be much easier to achieve than doing so by land or sea, I had not as yet fully travelled around the world by plane. I had flown with Leo in 1970 from London to Sydney and many times since then I had flown to and fro across the Atlantic Ocean to the USA and back. That meant that the two missing flights that would complete the journey by air around the World were (1) a flight across the Pacific, and (2) a flight or flights fully across the USA. I began to plan to make good this omission.

It wasn't going to be a cheap flight. The best way to achieve it was to travel all around the World, first by flying from London to Bangkok, then on to Sydney, then from Sydney across the Pacific Ocean to San Francisco. After stopping in San Francisco for a while I planned first to fly to New Mexico followed by a flight to Washington before catching the last of the planes back to London. I started to save hard and determined that the departure would be in 2008.

Sadly as 2008 came around, I realised regrettably that I would have to miss a family wedding. My lovely niece Nadine in Mauritius was getting married to Stefan and the marriage was happening while I was on my journey. There was nothing I could do about it as my plans had been set in stone long before I had heard of the date of the marriage. Also what it meant was that I would have to say my farewells to my wife Fopin and our two children, Zoe and Maxim, off on their flight to Mauritius, leaving me alone for a few days in London before the time came for me to catch my flight to Bangkok.

On Saturday 16th August 2008 I caught my flight

THE END OF THE JOURNEY

BA009 from Heathrow Terminal 4 at 22:00. The journey time to Thailand was 11:15 hours but because the time difference from the UK was six hours the plane arrived in Bangkok at 15:15 well into Sunday afternoon. At the airport I took a taxi to my hotel, the Plaza Athenee Bangkok.

The Plaza Athenee Bangkok had been booked for me by Chalin, the niece of Tham, my former neighbour in Wimbledon. Not only had she booked it for me but she had managed to get me a discount on the cost. Thanks so much Chalin!

At the hotel I met not only Chalin and her sister Bom but also my former neighbour Ted and a lovely lady called Boh who apparently had volunteered to drive us around Bangkok whilst I was there. That evening the five of us went to the Secret Garden Restaurant for a great welcoming meal.

After the meal, although it was a dark night, my body said that it was only afternoon causing me great difficulty in getting to sleep. In fact I only managed two hours sleep before I had to get up to meet up with Ted and Boh for my first day of sightseeing.

The day was very hot as we visited the Grand Palace and the Reclining Buddha. In the evening I reciprocated the previous night's hospitality by buying everybody a meal at the Aroy Dee Mee Hang fish restaurant. The day ended with shopping at the Night Market. That night I did slightly better than the previous night with four hours sleep, though still not a full night!

Tuesday the 19th August was to be my last day in Thailand so Ted and Boh took me out for a morning's sightseeing. The first place seen was the palace of the Crown Prince (who has just been made King as I write this in 2019!). After that we went to view the Old Parliament and the New Parliament before turning the car around to head back to my hotel. Suddenly I was a bit worried when we were abruptly brought to a halt by soldiers monitoring an industrial dispute. Apparently it meant that we could no longer return to my hotel the way that we had come. However Boh came good. She enquired of a policeman what alternative route we could use to get back to my hotel. He was able to help and finally Boh was able to drop me at my hotel. I thanked Ted and Boh profusely and dashed in to get ready for my trip to the airport.

At my hotel I quickly freshened up and paid my hotel bill before setting off in a taxi to take me to the airport. Worryingly my journey was being delayed yet again, this time by a protest outside the British Embassy by people demanding the extradition from Britain of the former Thai Prime Minister Thaksin Shinawatra. Somehow my taxi

THE END OF THE JOURNEY

driver got me to the airport in time for me to catch my flight to Sydney!

I caught the Qantas flight at 18:10 which landed in Sydney at 06:10 on the 20th August. Disturbingly though when I went to collect my luggage it was nowhere to be seen and I thought it had been lost. Finally however I found it—somehow it had been routed to the wrong carousel!

I was met by Leo and Laurie and after leaving the airport we stopped off to see my Oz mother, Laurie's mum, before moving on to Leo's home in Marsfield.

Unfortunately I was not in good physical condition. Apart from being tired because of the bad sleep, I was also croaky and had blood shot eyes which turned out to be conjunctivitis that had not been diagnosed at an opticians back in Wimbledon shortly before I left.

Despite the poor sleep that I had had on the journey so far, I still had trouble sleeping due to all the changing time zones and two planes. I chilled the next day watching the Beijing Olympics while Leo went to work. In the evening we went for dinner at a local Italian restaurant.

The next day despite only having gone to sleep at 04:00 I travelled with Leo to his office in the City after which I walked back over Darling Harbour checking out old places I knew until I met up with Leo and Laurie near the Sydney

Town Hall. After lunch, whilst Leo resumed work, I went with Laurie to visit his new flat in Mosman. At 21:00 Leo picked me up and we returned to his flat.

My eyes were getting worse so, on the good advice of my friend Ian Bowie, I was taken to an eye clinic at McQuarie Shopping Centre where I got treatment for my eyes for $55 and purchased an eye ointment which immediately led to improvement.

On Sunday the 24th August I went with Leo by car to Canberra to meet up with Peter and Sally Parsons. We were taken out for an excellent lunch at the Canberra Hotel where we were joined by their son Simon and a Welsh friend Richard. On the way back to Sydney I was dropped off at Laurie's for the night during which I was able to watch the Closing Ceremony of the Olympics. After that I still could not sleep until 05:00 eventually waking at 10:30.

Later that morning Laurie and I made our way into the city to meet up with not only Leo but two other mates Brian Davoren and Dennis Hale.

A couple of days later I met up with my old flatmate Mike Stephenson with his wife Paula, their daughter Jodie and their granddaughter Hannah. When we were joined by Leo and Ian, Mike took us to the Bowlers Club for an excellent smorgasbord lunch.

THE END OF THE JOURNEY

Thursday the 28th was an exciting day because I had an appointment to meet Donna Newton, the librarian at The Royal Australian Historical Society in McQuarie Street. Donna gave me a tour around the Society during which my book *Cast Into The Unknown*, that described the ten years that I had lived in Australia, was placed in the Library. I had become part of Australian history! After this I was joined by my publisher Rosa and another former colleague Liz Pring and I bought the three of us lunch at an Italian restaurant.

At this time big things were happening in the USA and on the next day the democratic presidential candidate, Barrack Obama, was making a speech to the nation. Shortly after watching this I had my first proper sleep in Sydney waking at 05:00. In the evening I had my last meal with Nick and Zuria before being driven back to Leo's house at Marsfield.

The next day, Sunday 31st August, Leo drove me to the airport where I caught the 13:55 flight to San Francisco. I was lucky to find myself sharing three seats with a lady called Donna McDonald returning to her home and family in California after a short holiday in Australia. Donna was good company and the long journey over the Pacific seemed to pass very quickly, in fact time disappeared! For example we left Sydney at 13:55 on Sunday afternoon and arrived in San Francisco at 10:00 Sunday morning! We seemed to have lost over a day in the flight. **Nevertheless when we landed at San Francisco I had completed my first flight across the Pacific Ocean!**

At San Francisco I was met by my nephew Kwong who kindly took me to a Korean restaurant for lunch before taking me on a drive around San Francisco by way of introduction to this lovely city. Following that, after a little supermarket shopping, we made our way to his flat to chill out before enjoying a great Mongolian buffet meal in the evening. San Francisco was proving a great place to enjoy food!

The next day we drove to the famous Golden Gate Bridge where we parked the car for a while as we walked to the middle of the bridge. After that we drove for a short while before we caught a train called the Muni to the enormous Chinatown where we enjoyed a dim sum lunch. Afterwards a BART train took us to Dolores Park where we met up with a large group of Kwong's friends relaxing on the grass in the strong sunshine.

In the evening I met up with more friends of Kwong at his flat where Kwong, who is well known as a great cook, cooked a meal for all of us. Joseph, Tina, Amanda, Belinda, and of course myself, enjoyed this repast.

THE END OF THE JOURNEY

Despite the meal I was still having troubling sleeping properly, I had had barely any sleep since leaving London! It was only when I eventually got back to London that I discovered why I had been having this trouble. In one of the daily newspapers there was a question and answer section. Someone had written in to say that they experienced the same difficulty sleeping on planes that I had just had, and asked what could be done about. In answer, an air stewardess suggested that one should try, if possible, to travel around the World flying from the east to the west. This was of course the opposite of what I had been doing and I would have slept better if instead I had flown first from London to the USA returning later to London from Bangkok.

The next morning Kwong returned to work leaving me to my own resources. I decided to catch the Muni to Powell where I got the legendary cable car to the waterfront. From there I caught a tour vehicle which introduced me to much more of this lovely city.

On my last day in San Francisco I made a second visit to Chinatown where I found an excellent restaurant in Jackson Street before meeting Kwong's friend Joseph for some drinks. In the evening Kwong and I were invited for dinner at the flat of Katherine, Mon and Jenny, lovely young ladies that I had met in Dolores Park a few days earlier.

The next day I was leaving San Francisco and California to head for New Mexico. I woke at 07:00 after another poor sleep and Kwong drove me to the airport where I caught the 11:46 plane to Albuquerque. When I arrived there I looked in vain for my brother-in-law Randy. When Randy eventually arrived it transpired that there had been some change in arrival time since I had given them to him. It was good to see Randy and we drove for about an hour to Sorocco where I met yet another of Fopin's lovely sisters, his wife Nachin. Randy and Nachin had met in Madagascar in 1969 when Randy was working on perhaps the most dramatic project of the 20th century, putting the first man on the Moon.

The next morning was an exciting day for me as Randy took me to where he worked at the VLA (Very Large Array) where I was able to sight 27 massive antennae searching the Universe for signs of alien life. We met up with Nachin later at a barbeque that she was sharing with some of her colleagues from the school where Nachin was a teacher.

The next day was possibly even more dramatic. First of all Randy, Nachin and I drove to Lincoln where William Bonney (Billy The Kid) shot and killed two lawmen before being shot dead himself. Then, after a roadside picnic lunch, we drove to Roswell the township where the aliens allegedly crashed on the 7th of July 1947. I didn't get to see the site of the crash but I did visit the International UFO Centre where I bought one book and was bought a second book by Randy on this fascinating subject.

The next day there was more excitement when we went to see the home of the Pueblo Indians in Frijoles Canyon and later to the town of Los Alamos where the Atomic Bomb was developed in the 1930s and 1940s.

Two days later Randy and I left at 06:40 to drive to Albuquerque where I caught the 10:00 plane for a three-hour and-30 minute journey to Washington. Even though the plane arrived there 20 minutes early I was met on exit by Randy and Nachin's lovely daughter Debbie, accompanied by her two children Ben and Grace. Debbie drove us to her home where we were joined later by her husband Paul. That night we feasted on some lovely cooking by Debbie after which it was necessary for her and her family to hit the hay. The children were very young and needed to get their beauty sleep and Debbie herself, being a school teacher, had also to get some rest so that she would be ready for an early start the next day.

I was shown to my bedroom in the basement of the house where I decided to send off a few emails before deciding to turn on the television to see what was happening in the presidential election that was taking place at this time. I was lucky as the broadcast turned out to be gripping stuff. Obama's opponent, Senator John McCain of Arizona had announced that his vice presidential running mate was to be a lady with the name Governor Sarah Palin of Alaska. After watching the speeches etc for a good hour or more, I finally relented and went to bed after 23:00, fell immediately into a deep sleep, and in so doing had the best sleep that I had had since leaving London.

The next morning I joined Paul as he went on the train to work. I left him as we entered the Washington Centre where I got off and went on a walking tour of the city seeing the White House, the Washington Monument, the Reflecting Pond and the Lincoln Memorial. All this walking made me very hungry so I decided I should go to the Washington Chinatown where I found myself an excellent meal at the Chinatown Express on 6th Street. After lunch I found my way back to the family home in Braddock Road where I accompanied Debbie and the kids to the local park before enjoying another evening meal.

The next day was Thursday the 11th September, the day I was due to catch my final flight back to London. In the morning I saw a little more of the Capital before relaxing until the evening when I was driven by Paul to the airport.

THE END OF THE JOURNEY

Many thanks to Debbie and Paul for a lovely end to my journey.

I arrived back in London nearly one month after leaving there and in so doing **I had completed a journey by plane all around the World.**

This also marked the end of the journey that I had started way back in 1961. In that journey I had completed a journey around the world by sea in 1971, completed a worldwide journey by land in 2003, and finally completed flying around the world by air in 2008.

The end of my journey ... though not of my travels!

THE END

Acknowledgements

My thanks to my lovely wife Fopin and my two great children Zoe and Maxim for being so patient with me and my itchy feet.

Thanks to my sister Sylvia for her help and advice during the writing and publishing of this book.

Many thanks to my long-time Aussie friend Leo Detsikas for his companionship on the longest rail journey in the world and now for writing such an excellent Foreword.

Thanks to my friends Paul Evans and Chris Chinnery for providing me their technical support in this endeavour.

Immense appreciation to my nephew Kwong Li for his great expertise in drawing the wonderful maps that illustrate my travels so vividly.

Thanks to my three long-time friends Tony Gomersal, Graham Craik and William Karunairajan for their friendship and encouragement during my travel years.

And, of course, finally many thanks to my excellent publisher, James Harrison of Oxfordfolio.